Care of the Elderly Mentally Infirm

BARBARA GRAY
& BERNARD ISAACS

Tavistock Publications
LONDON AND NEW YORK

First published in 1979 by
Tavistock Publications Ltd
11 New Fetter Lane, London EC4P 4EE
Published in the USA by
Tavistock Publications
in association with Methuen, Inc.
733 Third Avenue, New York, NY 10017

© 1979 Barbara Gray and Bernard Isaacs

Filmset in Great Britain by
Northumberland Press Ltd,
Gateshead, Tyne and Wear
Printed by
The University Press,
Cambridge

ISBN 0 422 77190 2   (hardback edition)
ISBN 0 422 77180 5   (paperback edition)

British Library Cataloguing in Publication Data

Gray, Barbara, b. date
    Care of the elderly mentally infirm.
    1. Mentally ill – Care and treatment
    – Great Britain
    2. Aged – Great Britain – Care and hygiene
    I. Title   II. Isaacs, Bernard, b. date
    362.6′12′0941   RC451.4.A5   79–40801

    ISBN 0–422–77190–2
    ISBN 0–422–77180–5 Pbk

Care of the Elderly Mentally Infirm

CONTENTS

'*Warning*' *Jenny Joseph*   vii

Foreword   ix

1 Characteristics of the Elderly Mentally Infirm (*B. I.*)   1

2 An Outline of Mental Illness in the Elderly (*B. I.*)   5

3 The Symptoms of Brain Failure (*B. I.*)   16

4 Other Mental Illness (*B. I.*)   30

5 Normal and Abnormal Personality (*B. I.*)   43

6 The National Health Service and the Elderly Mentally Infirm (*B. I.*)   49

7 Demographic and Social Aspects of Old Age (*B. G.*)   62

8 Social Services for the Elderly (*B. G.*)   80

9 Communicating with Elderly People (*B. G.*)   101

10 Social Work Intervention (*B. G.*)   112

11 Needs of Relatives (*B. G.*)   133

12 A Better Future? (*B. G.* and *B. I.*)   147

Appendix 1 Legislation   161

Appendix 2 Brief Legal Notes   169

Appendix 3 Financial Concessions   171

Appendix 4 Guidelines for Social Workers   174

      (a) Symptoms of Mild and Severe Intrinsic Brain Failure and of Extrinsic Brain Failure   174

      (b) Assessment of Elderly Client at Risk in the Community   175

      (c) Guidelines for Communicating with Elderly People   182

(d) Problems Faced by Carers and Possible Solutions 183

(e) Helping to Keep Old People in the Community 185

Appendix 5 Key Addresses 187

Appendix 6 Voluntary Social Services 189

Appendix 7 Mrs Sarah Merton, Aged 87, A Client at Risk 190

Appendix 8 Brief Case Studies for Discussion 196

Appendix 9 Additional Tables 199

Glossary 201

References 206

Index 217

WARNING

Jenny Joseph

When I am an old woman I shall wear purple
With a red hat which doesn't go, and doesn't suit me
And I shall spend my pension on brandy and summer gloves
And Satin sandals, and say we've no money for butter.
I shall sit down on the pavement when I'm tired
And gobble up samples in shops and press alarm bells
And run my stick along the public railings
And make up for the sobriety of my youth.
I shall go out in my slippers in the rain
And pick the flowers in other people's gardens
And learn to spit.

You can wear terrible shirts and grow more fat
And eat three pounds of sausages at a go
Or only bread and pickle for a week
And hoard pens and pencils and beermats and things in
boxes.

But now we must have clothes that keep us dry
And pay rent and not swear in the street
And set a good example for the children
We must have friends to dinner and read the papers.

But maybe I ought to practise a little now?
So people who know me are not too shocked and surprised
When suddenly I am old and start to wear purple.

FOREWORD

This book is addressed primarily to community social workers involved in the care of the mentally infirm elderly. We hope that it will also be of interest to hospital social workers and nursing staff in general, geriatric, and psychiatric wards and day hospitals; to caring and administrative staff of residential homes and day centres; to health visitors, community nurses, and voluntary helpers; indeed to all those whose work or whose ordinary human concern brings them into contact with this unhappy group of people and leaves them with the feeling that there must be something more that can be done to help. We would feel especially gratified if the relatives, neighbours, and friends of the mentally infirm elderly were to find the book helpful. They receive little enough help in their uniquely difficult task of caring.

The book is written against the background of the British National Health Service and Social Services, which provide the framework for service delivery in the United Kingdom. No matter how well-motivated a social worker is, the most effective way to help the client is to understand and operate the system. Readers who are unfamiliar with the British network of services will doubtless find many similarities with their own countries in the fundamental nature of the problem and in the responses which it evokes.

Throughout the book social workers and old people have normally been described as 'she' and doctors as 'he'. No sex prejudice is intended. It is merely a device to avoid clumsy repetition and to save ambiguity.

In writing this book Barbara Gray and Bernard Isaacs were

greatly assisted by colleagues with intimate knowledge of day-to-day work with mentally infirm elderly clients. The medical author is not a psychiatrist, but was most fortunate in his close collaboration throughout the writing of the book with Professor Andrew Sims. Professor Sims, in addition to helping with Chapters 2 and 3, provided all the material on which Chapters 4 and 5 are based.

Miss Ruth Wilkes, Social Work Tutor at East Birmingham Hospital, played a similar role in relation to the social work author. Miss Wilkes' wide knowledge of social work, her keen intelligence, and independent and ironic viewpoint illuminate the social work section, particularly Chapters 8 and 10.

Other colleagues gave information and criticisms. The late Dr Dermot Mahon gave valuable information on the statutory background. Neil Thomas and Marie Willard helped with aspects of residential care and Jean Glover and Stephen Nixon with fieldwork. Mr Ronald Liddiard and his staff made useful suggestions about the content of Chapter 8, to which Mrs Maureen Pearson also contributed. Mr John Davies advised on the content of brief legal notes. Dr Mark Abrams gave information which greatly strengthened Chapter 7.

We wish also to thank Jenny Joseph for permission to print her poem; Professor Grimley Evans for allowing us to reproduce *Table 5* in Chapter 7 and Her Majesty's Stationery Office for permission to quote selected statistical data from official publications.

Last, but not least, we would like to thank Mrs Jean Yetman and Mrs Valerie Kedge for typing the manuscript.

To all those who contributed, and particularly to Professor Sims and Miss Wilkes, the authors owe a great debt. The errors in the book they acknowledge as their own, but are grateful for the time and effort devoted by others to trying to reduce these to a minimum.

1 CHARACTERISTICS OF THE ELDERLY MENTALLY INFIRM

Two illustrative cases

The doctor was called because Mrs Williamson had walked down the road in the nude. Mrs Williamson was 87 and it was mid November. She wasn't exactly in the nude, but all that she was wearing was a tattered old dressing-gown, devoid of buttons or belt. Her neighbours had dealt with this behaviour many times before, but this time they felt that something more had to be done and the doctor was called. He said there was nothing he could do about it but he would call a specialist. He was undecided whether to call a psychiatrist or a geriatrician but chose the latter. When the geriatrician came to the house, one of a row of pensioners' bungalows in a quiet side street, he found the patient lying in bed. The door was opened by a shame-faced, dishevelled man in his mid sixties. This was the patient's only son. His home was three miles away in another part of the town. He had had to give up work two years previously after suffering a coronary thrombosis and he lived on sickness benefit and his wife's earnings as a cleaner. He visited the patient twice a week and stayed overnight in the house because he couldn't afford the bus fare in both directions more often. He slept on an old army camp bed on the floor. On each of the other three days of the week one of his three daughters – all married and all living in different and distant parts of the city – found time between attending to their jobs, their children, and their husbands to call and keep an eye on the old lady. But most of the time she was on her own, and she would not allow anyone else in the house – neighbours, friends, home-help, health visitors, meals-on-wheels, voluntary workers, or anyone.

The stripping was of recent occurrence and seemed quite inexplicable. The old lady was oblivious alike of cold, embarrassment, and reprimand. Her sallies forth took place at all times of the day and in all weathers, sometimes two or three times in one day. She got out of bed and went to the door while her son was telling the geriatrician about this. The son was not hardened to the situation and he averted his gaze as the dressing-gown opened out in front. The old lady sat down and found an old cigarette end somewhere, pulled a piece of paper tissue out of a box, held the tissue in front of the ancient electric bar fire until it burst into flames, lit the cigarette incredibly slowly with a shaking hand while the flames licked at her thinning eyebrows, then tossed the still burning tissue on to the floor in grand unconcern. She did not speak throughout these proceedings – indeed she seldom said anything. She was short, fat, pale, and pasty, but extremely agile in her movements. She was dirty, her hair was bedraggled, and her eyes were wild. Her fingernails were stained and the soles of her bare feet were black. She took a few puffs of her cigarette butt, threw it away and clambered back into bed.

Her son explained that he had first noticed that her memory was becoming impaired some seven or eight years previously, but she had coped well with life until her husband's death three years later. It was then that she had become what he looked upon as 'a bit queer'. She grew more argumentative, disliked company, and stopped visiting and being visited by her neighbours and friends. She neglected her personal cleanliness and probably was not feeding herself properly but would not have any help from anyone. Her son noted that when she spoke she had a tendency to 'ramble'. Then, several months previously, the dog that had been her only companion was killed in a street accident. 'That', said the son, 'broke the cord'. Her wandering had begun, her self-neglect had become more extreme, her speech had become less and less coherent. Eventually she began to wander off in the nude shocking her neighbours who made contact with her local doctor.

DIFFERENT MANIFESTATIONS OF THE SAME DISEASE
Mr Walter Schulz was 65, an immigrant in his boyhood, who by dint of ambition, hard work, and astuteness had built up a very considerable commercial enterprise. He was a wealthy man, chairman and managing director of his own company, of which the other directors included his brother and his two sons. He ran the show;

the business was his creation. Then he began to make errors of judgement. He bought too much and he paid too much for it. He made ambitious plans for the extension of the business which were extravagant and unrealistic. Never an easy man, he became highly intolerant of criticism and advice and ceased to consult anyone about his doings. His brother and his sons were incensed at his behaviour and concerned for the profitability of the business. They decided that the only way out was to call in a doctor and certify him as medically unfit to carry on. The doctor immediately detected that the patient was suffering from gross loss of recent memory and referred him to a psychiatrist who diagnosed the presence of brain failure and succeeded in persuading the patient to enter hospital.

COMPARISON OF THE CASES

The brains of each of these patients were undergoing damage by a progressive and destructive pathological process (see Chapter 2). The disease was the same but the brains were different. Mrs Williamson's was used largely for the performance of the mundane functions of a humble life, while Mr Schulz's was highly trained to take critical decisions affecting its owner and many others. The highly skilled brain was highly vulnerable to damage. Mr Schulz's errors of judgement harmed other people who quickly retaliated, by bringing the health care system to bear upon the problem. Mrs Williamson's brain was left to wither, slowing depriving its owner of any worthwhile existence. Only in the latest stages of the disease was such a threat posed to the physical safety and sense of propriety of others as to instigate action. In neither case was the doctor called in to deal medically with these symptoms. Both doctors were expected to use their authority in order to relieve relatives and neighbours of the harmful consequences of the patient's altered behaviour. Neither patient profited from the available services in the way that was intended. Mrs Williamson, having refused all types of hospital and domiciliary care, died at home suddenly and unexpectedly before she had caused a conflagration. Mr Schulz, after being persuaded to enter hospital for 'observation' sustained a myocardial infarction while inside.

Not all cases resemble these, and in other instances, to be presented later, effective collaboration between medical and social work services brought timely and effective care to the patient (see Chapter 10 and Appendix 7, pp.190–5).

Features of mental illness in the elderly

These two cases illustrate the differing clinical picture of mental illness during the thirty- or forty-year span of late life; and at various points in the economic, education, and intellectual scale. Mr Schulz with higher intellectual attainment and more complex involvement in society was more socially vulnerable to the effects of brain damage. Mrs Williamson illustrated the accumulation of physical and mental disease that is often a feature of extreme old age. Both patients exemplified the interaction between physical and mental illness, the loss of responsibility for the consequences of their own behaviour, and the social disruptiveness of this loss. Both showed how long it takes for the aberrations of behaviour, which are a feature of mental infirmity in late life, to be recognized as disease and for treatment to be sought. Both illustrated the lack of definition of which branch of the health and social services should accept responsibility for the care of this group. These matters will be considered in the following chapters.

2 AN OUTLINE OF MENTAL ILLNESS IN THE ELDERLY

In this chapter the main diseases, disorders, and disabilities which are included under the heading of 'mental infirmity' or 'mental illness' in the elderly will be briefly described. A glossary will be found at page 201. A more detailed description of symptoms and management follows in later chapters.

Definition of mental infirmity in the elderly

The terms 'the elderly with mental infirmity' (EMI) and 'the elderly with severe mental infirmity' (ESMI) appear in policy statements from the Department of Health and Social Security but are little used in the medical literature. They appear to have been introduced as euphemisms, and their connotation is imprecise. They convey the erroneous impression that mental illness in old age is uniform in nature and varies only in degree. This false impression must be quickly dispelled. In this book all kinds of mental illness in the elderly will be dealt with other than longstanding mental illness originating in earlier life and persisting uninterruptedly into old age.

While much 'mental infirmity' in old age is due to irreversible organic brain disease, this is by no means true of all mental illness in late life. The term 'mental infirmity' includes other forms of mental illness, many of which are eminently treatable.

MENTAL NORMALITY

Normal old people, like normal people of any other age, show a wide range of intellectual capacity, emotional expression, and personality. These change in later life because of altered life

5

experience and social roles, to which are added, in some cases, the development of structural abnormality in the brain. Mental function may also be adversely affected by sensory deprivation and emotional change. Deafness, blindness, restriction of mobility, and depression cut off the victim from primary sources of information and from social participation, and thereby have an effect on the level of intellectual activity.

Loss of memory and concentration are so common in old people as to be considered 'normal for age'. However geriatricians, with special knowledge of and commitment to old people, argue that any deviation from the standards of earlier life is 'abnormal', though not necessarily sinister. They tend to reject the concept of 'normal for age' because it is so often used to cloak early and possibly treatable abnormality. The argument is not merely about the meaning of words. Insidious alterations in intellect or behaviour may be early signs of treatable disease. It is better to recognize and accept deviations from the normal, and then to decide whether they need cause anxiety or require treatment.

DEFINITIONS

The following statements are not so much formal definitions as descriptions of the assumptions on which the argument in this book is based.

Mental abnormality means deviation from the level of intellectual performance, emotional range, or personality pattern characteristic of the subject in earlier life.

Mental illness means deviation of such severity as to cause concern and anxiety in the subject or in others close to the subject.

TYPES OF MENTAL ABNORMALITY

It is convenient to think of three main categories of mental abnormality: disturbances of intellect, of mood, and of personality respectively. This is an artificial distinction since the three aspects frequently co-exist and interact with one another; and since one or more is often accompanied by physical illness, disability, or social disadvantage. But the categorization is a useful one and allows for systematic presentation.

INTELLECTUAL FUNCTION

It is widely believed that intellect normally declines with age. Earlier experimental studies, which were thought to give support to this belief, demonstrated that if people of different ages were given standardized psychological tests to perform, the older ones were less successful than the younger ones (see Savage *et al.* (1973); Bromley (1974); Heron and Chown (1967). This type of experiment, which is called a 'cross-sectional study' is subject to many fallacies. Different people, of different educational and cultural backgrounds, are given the same test at the same time. The older ones are likely to be more difficult to recruit into such studies than the younger ones, and thus are more highly selected. They are also selected in that they are survivors of their generation. On the other hand they have by and large come from a more deprived background and experienced less exposure to education in their formative years. They are more likely to by physically ill and to be readily fatigued, and they may be bewildered by the task and reluctant to try to do their best.* Tests in which the same task is required of the same people at different ages are known as 'longitudinal studies'. These are obviously more difficult to organize and require a long time for the accumulation of data, but such tests as have been done tend to show that the decline of intellect with old age is very much less than was formerly believed, and that in many aspects intellectual function remains stable or even improves over the years. (The work of K. W. Schaie in this field is well presented in Hendricks and Hendricks (1977).) In particular, when old people are highly motivated by anxiety or personal interest intellectual performance may be excellent (Welford 1975). For example, many old people are remarkably knowledgeable about the complexities of the Social Security system or about the price of food in different shops.

THE NATURE OF INTELLECTUAL DECLINE IN OLD AGE

Epidemiological studies of random samples of the elderly population do however show that some 10 per cent of those aged 65 and over living in their own homes can be classed as intellectually impaired, and in about half of these the intellectual impairment is severe (see Kay, Beamish, and Roth 1964, 1965). The prevalence of mental impairment increases with increase of age. The figure is

---

* Mental test scores on hospital patients are lower than those found in people with an apparently comparable degree of intellectual function living at home. Very poor mental test performance may be predictive of early death. See for example Grimley Evans (1979).

quite low in those aged 65 to 74, much higher in those aged 75 to 84, and very high in those aged 85 and over. Exact prevalence figures for mental abnormality in old age depend on the criteria adopted by the investigator; but even when lay observers with no special training are used, prevalence figures, particularly in the oldest age groups, are still high. The minimum estimate is that there are a quarter of a million old people in the United Kingdom with quite severe intellectual impairment.

PATHOLOGICAL EVIDENCE
Post mortem examination of the brains of old people who have been mentally abnormal in late life reveals gross structural changes, which are described on pages 10–13. Similar finding of less severity are present in the brains of a high proportion of very old people who come to post mortem examination, and there is good correlation between the severity and extent of the pathological changes and the patient's behaviour and intellectual status in life (see Tomlinson 1977).

Terminology

Reference has already been made to the dangers of imprecision in terminology. Not only are many words used in this field vague, they are also highly charged emotionally. For example, the term 'senility' instantly conjures up an image of degradation and dilapidation, of physical, mental, and social degeneration, for which nothing can or should be done. Yet this word corresponds to no definable clinical condition. It should be said of no patient that he or she 'is suffering from senility'. Such people are suffering from the failure of others to identify and treat their illness. The adjective 'senile', when used alone, carries a similar connotation. Both these words should be avoided. There are some medical senses in which the word 'senile' is used to qualify another word, when its meaning is fairly precise and useful: e.g. the term 'senile vaginitis' applies to a particular form of a specific disease which is due to the hormonal changes of late life.

The word 'confusion' is widely used by non-psychiatrists to describe the faulty behaviour of the elderly with mental illness. Mentally ill old people frequently are unsure about their location in time and place and about the identity of their companions. In that sense the word 'confusion' is correctly used; although the terms 'disorientation' and 'delusions' are more precise. Less correctly the word 'confusion' is used to describe the disease which gave rise to the symptom. But confusion is not a disease; it is a manifestation of a number of diseases, which may be short-lived and reversible or long-lived and irreversible.

DEMENTIA

Confusion is a symptom, not a disease; dementia is a disease, not a symptom. It has given rise to two verbal participles, 'demented', apparently representing the end process of the disease, and 'dementing', taken to refer to an earlier stage in a progressive process. These words will be used only rarely in this book. 'Dementia' like 'senility' tends to carry negative connotations. Moreover the term is used to describe both the clinical syndrome of intellectual impairment and the pathological changes in the brain responsible for that syndrome. It is better to call the clinical syndrome 'brain failure' (Isaacs and Caird 1976).

CEREBRAL ARTERIOSCLEROSIS

The term 'cerebral arteriosclerosis' means hardening of the arteries of the brain. Such hardening does occur but is not responsible of itself for brain failure in the elderly. In vascular brain failure the brain is damaged as a result of disease in its blood vessels, but that disease is not properly described as 'cerebral arteriosclerosis'. In non-vascular brain failure the cause has nothing to do with blood vessels. The indiscriminate use of the term 'cerebral arteriosclerosis' as equivalent to brain failure is misleading, and raises the expectation that treatment directed towards the blood vessels may be effective.

The concept of brain failure

The clinical syndrome of impaired intellect in old age is described in this book by the term 'brain failure'. This expression is analagous to 'heart failure' or 'kidney failure'. It implies a syndrome with recognizable features which can result from different pathological processes. The term specifically implies that a diagnosis has not yet been made. Once the cause of the brain failure is established, the doctor should qualify the term by indicating the type of brain failure to which he alludes.

9

'FOCAL' AND 'DIFFUSE' DISEASE

Brain failure results from diffuse disease affecting the whole brain or many different parts of the brain. The term is not used to describe the syndromes resulting from 'discrete' lesions of the brain, for example tumour, abscess, or stroke.

TYPES OF BRAIN FAILURE

There are two main types of brain failure, (*Figure 1*), intrinsic and extrinsic and there are two main types of intrinsic brain failure, vascular and non-vascular.

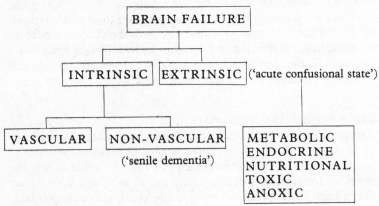

Figure 1

Intrinsic and extrinsic

In *intrinsic brain failure* ('dementia') the function of the whole brain is impaired by diffuse structural disease.

In *extrinsic brain failure* ('confusional state') the function of the whole brain is impaired by disease originating outside the brain.

Intrinsic and extrinsic brain failure may co-exist. Patients with intrinsic brain failure who suffer from a concomitant physical illness potentially capable of impairing brain function appear to be particularly susceptible to the hazard of accompanying extrinsic brain failure.

INTRINSIC BRAIN FAILURE

Vascular and non-vascular brain failure in the elderly have in common the following features:

(i) both are frequent in occurrence;
(ii) in both the damage is widespread throughout the brain;
(iii) the individual foci of disease are minute;
(iv) the amount of brain tissue destroyed is substantial;
(v) both are common in late life.

Not uncommonly the two diseases co-exist, but there is no causal connection between them.

The main distinguishing features are summarized in *Table 1*.

Table 1   *Intrinsic brain failure*

	vascular brain failure	*non-vascular brain failure*
age of onset	early 70s	late 70s
sex preference	slightly more common in men	much more common in women
relation to high blood pressure	close relationship	no relationship
relationship with other diseases	heart disease; peripheral arterial disease	no relationship
prognosis	many patients die of heart failure or stroke within a year or two of clinical presentation	patients may survive for many years especially if they enter hospital

Vascular brain failure
(*synonym 'arteriosclerotic dementia'*)
In vascular brain failure the brain is damaged by numerous small haemorrhages, or by blood clots which have formed in the brain or been carried through the bloodstream from a clot in the arteries of the neck or the wall of the heart. The blood supply of the affected area of the brain is cut off and the part dies. In advanced cases the brain is riddled with these small dead areas and much of its substance is destroyed. Occasionally a larger area of brain death results from a major haemorrhage or clot. The formation of such an area is associated with a distinct clinical event, e.g. a small stroke.

Non-vascular brain failure
(*synonym 'senile dementia'*)
The most common type of non-vascular brain failure in the elderly is a condition known under a variety of names, including 'senile

11

dementia', to which reference has already been made on page 9, 'Alzheimer's disease', and 'senile plaque disease'. This is characterized by the slow development over many years of large numbers of abnormal structures, visible only under the microscope, which are called 'senile plaques' and 'neurofibrillary tangles'. These disturb the connections between neighbouring nerve cells and progressively impair the ability of the brain to function as a whole. These changes are even found in small numbers in middle-aged people, especially in that area of the brain thought to play an important part in recent memory. This may explain the tendency of the middle-aged to be slightly forgetful. As the years progress the plaques and tangles increase in number and are found in other parts of the brain, particularly in the cortex. In most people they never become very numerous, and these people do not develop clinically significant symptoms. A few show rapid progression and extension of the disease, which becomes clinically apparent while they are still middle-aged. To this condition the term 'pre-senile dementia' is sometimes applied. More usually the extension of the pathological process is delayed until the eighth or ninth decades in life, and it is then that the clinical features become manifest.

Other diseases may be responsible for non-vascular brain failure in late life. The differentiation of these conditions is a matter for the specialist, who is on the alert for these cases in which some form of treatment is applicable.

Deaths in mental hospitals of brain failure

The non-vascular type accounts for more than half of such deaths; about one-third are of mixed disease; and in about one-sixth vascular brain failure is the sole cause (Corsellis 1962). This is contrary to the widely held view that most brain failure in the elderly is due to arterial disease.

Symptoms of intrinsic brain failure

In the non-vascular type the symptoms begin insidiously, with memory loss which is often attributed to old age itself. The condition advances slowly, sometimes over many years, until the more dramatic and disturbing manifestations, to be described in detail in the next chapter, are reached. The vascular type may begin with a more dramatic episode of disturbed behaviour or of abnormal neurological function. Thereafter there are periods of continuing deterioration, interspersed with periods of stability.

12

EXTRINSIC BRAIN FAILURE

The efficient working of the brain depends on a constant supply of fresh blood containing adequate oxygen and glucose, and free from toxic substances. Brain failure results from conditions which impede the free flow of blood, which provide insufficient oxygen or glucose, or which convey to the brain poisonous substances formed in or introduced into the body.

Many physical diseases exert these effects on the brain. For example, in pneumonia, the amount of oxygen conveyed by the blood is reduced; while poisonous substances produced by infecting bacteria further impair the functions of nerve cells.

Extrinsic brain failure may be caused by a large number of diseases, some of which are indicated in the table on page 11. The most common cause in daily clinical practice is probably the use of drugs prescribed for some other condition, which taken excessively, irregularly, or inappropriately are harmful to brain function. Other common causes include heart failure, infections, renal and liver disease, diabetes, the abuse of alcohol, respiratory disease, and various metabolic and endocrine conditions.

Symptoms

The primary illness becomes complicated with clouding of consciousness, delirium, drowsiness, or coma. Often the symptoms are florid, and the patient becomes noisy, hyperactive, anxious, frightened, and disturbed. There may be auditory or visual hallucinations or delusions. Speech may be highly excitable and fragmented, and there may be changes in bladder and bowel emptying. When the underlying physical disease is insidious in onset, for example thyroid disease, then the mental symptoms resemble those of intrinsic brain failure.

A mixed picture occurs when a patient with mild or unrecognized intrinsic brain failure suffers a new physical illness, such as myocardial infarction, and suddenly becomes much more severely mentally disturbed. Recovery from the physical illness may be accompanied by a return to the previous mental state; but sometimes mental recovery is incomplete and permanent deterioration ensues. The diagnosis of the cause of extrinsic brain failure is a matter for the doctor.

Emotional disorders

Progressive decline is no more the norm for the emotional life of

13

the elderly than it is for the intellectual life. The picture of the candle of the emotions flickering, burning low, and becoming extinguished is very far from the truth. The emotions of old people are intense, perhaps even more intense than of those who have yet to face old age. Old people are capable of great joy and great suffering; they experience depression, anxiety, and paranoia as at other times of life.

CONCEPTS OF NORMALITY

It is even more difficult to define the normal emotional state of late life than it is to indicate what is the normal intellectual state. Old people have much to be paranoid about, and it calls for nice judgement to determine when the sadness induced by loss of health, wealth, role, and companionship is to be expected, and when it trespasses into the area of pathology. Similar difficulties arise in interpreting fear of falling, burglary, or darkness and solitude. If an old person constantly reiterates a viewpoint, or behaves as though dominated and controlled by his emotions, these are signs of ill health. The subject will be dealt with in detail in Chapter 4.

PERSONALITY

The most intractable situations which doctors and social workers are called upon to unravel in old people are the manifestations of disordered personality. There is no identifiable disease which calls for treatment; instead there is emotional turmoil spreading from a source and extending widely to family, neighbours, and beyond. Often these disturbed personalities are the continuation into old age of a personality which has always been odd or unusual, and of which the eccentric characteristics have become exaggerated under the stresses of late life. It is probably less important to attempt to distinguish normal from abnormal personality than it is to recognize the source of the disturbance as being a manifestation of a personality disorder rather than of a mental illness. This is dealt with in greater detail in Chapter 5.

Summary

The many manifestations of mental illness in old age have been briefly described, in order to give to the social worker a medical overview of the field in which she is employed. A more detailed description of clinical syndromes follows in the ensuing chapters.

A recurring theme in this chapter, and throughout the book, is interaction of the different varieties of mental illness with one another and with physical, emotional, social, and personality factors.

3 THE SYMPTOMS OF BRAIN FAILURE (DEMENTIA)

The objects of this chapter are to describe and to interpret the behaviour of old people with brain failure, and to suggest methods of assessment and management.

Manifestations of brain failure
The manifestations of brain failure are very varied, depending on the pathological cause, the personality of the patient and the environmental situation. Nevertheless certain features are common to many patients.

A GENERAL FORMULATION
In very broad terms the manifestations of brain failure will be summarized thus:

   (i) a tendency to commit errors;
  (ii) a failure to perceive errors;
 (iii) a failure to comprehend the consequences of errors.

SEQUENCE OF EVENTS
The sequence of events in everyday situations facing patients with brain failure are conditioned by the following factors:

    (i) the personality of the patient;
   (ii) the demands of the task;
  (iii) the comprehension of the task;
  (iv) the repertoire of available behaviour;
   (v) the relative vulnerability of behaviour patterns;
  (vi) motivation in the choice of behaviour;

(vii) the consequences of that behaviour;
(viii) the patient's perception and comprehension of the consequences;
(ix) the response of those around;
(x) the further response which this elicits in the patient.

EXAMPLES OF THE BEHAVIOUR OF PATIENTS WITH BRAIN FAILURE

A list of the symptoms of mild and severe intrinsic brain failure and of extrinsic brain failure respectively is shown in Appendix 4(a). This list, although extensive, is not comprehensive; but most patients, if observed for long enough, show some of these manifestations.

Illustrative cases

Five commonly encountered clinical situations will be selected almost at random from the list of symptoms. Each will be briefly described and analysed, in an attempt to illustrate how these distressing events occur and how they might be managed. The situations to be dealt with are:

(i) the burned-out kettle;
(ii) the living dead;
(iii) 28lb. of sugar;
(iv) concealed underwear;
(v) wandering.

THE BURNED-OUT KETTLE

The patient puts a kettle on the stove, lights the gas, goes away, and forgets it, until the water boils away and the kettle is burned out. She leaves a pot of potatoes cooking, forgets it, the water boils dry, the potatoes are charred, and the pot burns out. She turns on the gas, goes to look for a match, forgets why she has gone, and leaves the gas on until the room is filled with gas. The neighbours are anxious and fearful lest a tragedy should occur. The patient is blandly indifferent.

Analysis

The mechanism is *diminished vigilance*, accompanied by failure to register recent events, especially in relation to self-initiated acts. Neither the error nor its consequences are perceived. The patient

17

fails to signal the fact that the room is filled with steam, smoke, or gas; or if she does perceive this she fails to attach significance to it. The patient is unable to traverse the gap in time between the present percept, i.e. a steam-filled room, and the preceding causal event, i.e. the boiling kettle. Nor will she have the foresight to appreciate that the vaporization of the water in the kettle will eventually lead to an empty kettle and the penetration of its base by the flame. The patient lacks any sense of personal responsibility for the event, which has become, as it were, detached from the act of the initiator. It is just a kettle boiling, existing independently in time and space.

Management
The obvious act of management is to introduce fail-safe devices, e.g. a kettle that automatically switches off when it boils, a safety gas cooker in which the gas ceases to flow if it is not ignited. Failing the provision of automatic safety devices, the 'signal level' can be increased by using a whistling kettle, but it may be found that the patient is impervious to the significance of this warning.

Attempts to restrain the patient from undertaking cooking may be self-defeating, arousing resentment and provoking denial of the dangers. Removal or concealment of kettles and cooking pots is a subterfuge which many families and neighbours feel compelled to adopt, but this can start off a prolonged cat and mouse conflict with the patient, which is better avoided.

This is a difficult situation, but much help can be obtained from the gas and electricity boards and from occupational therapists in trying to engineer safety. The objective is to leave the patient in a state of supervised independence in a reasonably secure environment, rather than to restrict her freedom of action. In this and in many similar situations there has to be willingness to accept some degree of risk and to try to minimize that risk, rather than to aim at the often unattainable objective of freedom from all danger.

THE LIVING DEAD
The patient speaks of her long-dead mother as though she were still alive, and describes how they went out shopping together that morning. In most other respects the patient appears to be fairly mentally normal.

Analysis

The patient is living in the past, in a sort of reverie, just as normal people often do, but unlike normal people she fails to distinguish reverie from reality. To her the dream *is* reality, and occupies the same place in her current picture of the world as do the objectively real events which surround her. She has a strong emotional motive for preserving the reality of her dream, and suppresses the apparent conflict between reverie and reality. If she is asked where her mother is now she 'confabulates' (see page 24) and says that she has gone into the next room. She says that her mother is 67, and admits that she herself is 68, but is unaware of the logical conflict. For her these two statements of age are independent, and each is in its own way true. If the conflict with reality is brought to her attention she 'denies' it, either explicitly by re-affirmation of what she believes to be the facts, or implicitly by the use of a phrase such as 'that's funny, isn't it?', unaccompanied by any change of mental set.

Management

Management is a matter of acceptance. The patient is in no way harmed, indeed she is cheered, by her delusion, and attempts to disturb it will in any case fail. Relatives may attempt to correct the delusion either in the belief that this helps the patient or because they are themselves distressed by references to a dead person. Relatives should be told firmly not to contradict.

28LB. OF SUGAR

The patient comes home from the grocer's with 28lb. of sugar. She had bought the same amount only one week ago. She does not need sugar. She cannot afford 28lb. of sugar. She has nowhere to put it. When questioned about it, she replies blandly, 'I like to have sugar in the house'.

Analysis

The patient is *perseverating* (see page 25) in a familiar behaviour pattern which has now outlived its former usefulness and relevance. Perseveration implies a failure to switch from an obsolete behaviour pattern to a more appropriate one. At one time she needed sugar and she bought it. Because her mind cannot move laterally into an assessment of her other needs, she finds it easier to continue to buy sugar. She can neither assess her needs realistically, nor can she foresee the consequences of her repetitive actions. She leaves the

19

house and makes for the grocer's shop with a desire to buy food, and she expresses this general desire in the one specific activity of purchasing sugar.

Management
By the time this pattern is established, attempts to remonstrate with the patient usually fail and should therefore be avoided. It is easier to explain the situation to the grocer and to seek his collaboration in some suitable exercise of deception, or in taking back surplus sugar when it can be spirited away without the patient's knowledge. Once again tension is generated when the family react as if the actions of the patient were those of a rational and responsible human being. Awareness of the nature of her disability and acceptance of the limitations of her comprehension avoid trouble.

CONCEALED UNDERWEAR
The patient, who has always been clean and fastidious, soils her underwear with urine and faeces. Instead of rinsing and laundering them, she wraps them in newspaper and hides them in the cutlery drawer, where they are subsequently found by a horrified daughter. The patient indignantly denies having put them there.

Analysis
Few symptoms give more offence or cause more distress than this one. The explanation is to be found in the patient's image of her own ego. She sees herself, as she always has done, as a clean, continent, and responsible person. When she finds the soiled underwear she has little or no recollection of having soiled it, and she cannot conceive of it as having been soiled by herself. She therefore 'detaches' the garment, soilage and all, from her body and from her body image. Once she has removed the underwear it no longer belongs to her. She accepts no responsibility for having soiled it or for having to clean it. She wraps it up and puts it out of sight, and quite firmly out of mind. She may hide the soiled package in one of her own drawers, but is just as likely to put it in the kitchen, which is neutral territory, to confirm that this was none of her doing. Her indignation at the subsequent accusations levelled against her is genuine and sincere. She may have no recollection of what she has done, but she is convinced that this is not the sort of thing that a person like her would do.

Management

The incontinence responsible for the incident requires medical attention. However, this act is the behaviour of those who are not really incontinent and in whom accidental soilage is occasional. It may be due to nothing more than constipation, relatively easily corrected. Progressive incontinence is accompanied by a reduction in the sense of shame and thus in reduced motivation for concealment.

WANDERING

The patient disappears from the house at night, clad only in a nightdress, and is found hours later miles away unable to account for how she got there.

Analysis

The restless urge to move and to search is deeply imbedded in the personality of many people. This need is met by the demands of many occupations, which involve travel and successful quests. Even taking the bus to work and opening the mail are part of the saga of voyage and discovery, while the more exotic careers of the mariner, the explorer, or the vagrant allow fuller expression of these human desires. Confinement to the four walls of a house, and loss of the familiar treasures of a lifetime, especially of loved ones, leaves the urge for voyage and discovery unfulfilled. Some are content just to sit and think, but others of different personality need to rise and wander off. So weak is the link of the patient suffering from brain failure with the realities of time and space around her that her wandering is seen as inappropriate and purposeless, offensive to the social demands of the environment, and hazardous to survival in a cold, dark world. An alternative explanation is that the wanderer is restlessly searching for her lost world.

Management

The urge to restrain and confine is often as strong in the relatives as is the urge to escape and be free in the patient. The conflict between these two urges is symbolized by the locked door and the tranquillizer. Locking doors is the natural reaction of one who fears the consequences of wandering, yet the locked door is bound to heighten the wanderer's frustration and resentment, and can lead to interminable banging and rattling. Sedative drugs are sometimes very beneficial and may be worth a judicious trial, but, as many

21

have discovered, they are often a poor solution. There are indeed few satisfactory solutions. The restless wanderer is a problem wherever she goes, whether in mental hospital and residential homes or in her own home. Some hospitals and homes provide garden areas, courtyards, or corridors in which wandering can occur without danger. Some offer a constant programme of activity, e.g. dancing and musical games to absorb the surplus energies of the patient. Some help by taking patients to public houses or private bars. These constructive measures can be very successful, but require higher staffing levels than are available in most homes and hospitals. For other patients it is at least arguable that their own homes are the best place for them, provided that the family can come to terms with the potential hazards. By the time an old person has so lost her awareness of the real world that she wanders restlessly and irresponsibly through it, some families accept that there can be worse things than a traffic accident. They dread even more the prospect that institutional care and separation may depersonalize and immobilize their loved one. Wandering presents to the carer a fearful dilemma – whatever is done appears to be wrong – and it is a relief when after months or years frailty deprives the patient of the ability to travel far.

Brain mechanisms
In this section the vulnerable brain mechanisms which are evident in brain failure, and which were illustrated in the preceding episodes, will be briefly described. Psychological texts should be consulted for more detailed presentation (see Williams 1970; Talland 1968).

REGISTRATION
The registration of new information is impaired in brain failure. Defective registration is manifest in the patient's inability to recall recently given information, to obey instructions, to keep records of her own actions. Patients read the newspaper, listen to the radio, or watch television without 'taking anything in'. Registration takes a long time, and a brief signal passes unrecorded. Only one item can be registered at a time, and only one channel of entry can be used. Registration is impaired at times of fatigue, e.g. in the late afternoon, and the capacity to register new information quickly becomes exhausted. Registration is reinforced by repetition. The great ease with which patients with brain failure appear to forget is largely due to their failure to register.

DISCRIMINATION

Patients with brain failure have impaired ability to distinguish significant differences between similar stimuli, and to discard non-significant similarities between different stimuli. For example, two people with the same colour of hair may be confused with one another, although they do not resemble each other in any other respect. Two people of different appearance but wearing a similar badge or uniform may not be recognized as belonging to the same set of people. Also lost in brain failure is the capacity to disregard what is irrelevant in the total sensory input to the particular business in hand. Normal people, in a crowded room, look at and listen to only one or two, and disregard the remainder. Patients with brain failure disconcert by joining in conversations not addressed to them.

Errors of visual discrimination can lead to accident or embarrassment. Patients may fail to distinguish the bottom of a flight of steps from the floor and fall in consequence; or they may be unable to see the difference in light and texture between the sleeve hole of a jumper and the remainder of the garment and thus have difficulty in dressing.

ABSTRACTION

Abstraction is the ability to draw general inferences from specific stimuli; to relate present events to past experience; to infer the underlying whole from the perceived part; to organize material in a hierarchical order; to relate present percepts to past experience; to exercise judgement based on previous knowledge. Normal people use this power of abstraction to give them information on time, place, the identity of persons around them, and the significance of their behaviour. Percepts are judged, assessed, and related to others. Tentative concepts are formed and remodelled as additional information is brought to bear. If a normal person's watch reads five to six and she hears Big Ben striking six o'clock, she deduces that her watch is slow. The patient with brain failure is more likely to conclude that Big Ben is fast, since she prefers her first percept and cannot discard it in favour of the more probable second percept.

Patients who lack the power of abstraction interpret the world in a 'concrete' manner, responding only to the immediate stimulus, as though they have lost access to the 'filing systems' of their brain.

ANTICIPATION

Normal people know what is likely to happen when a lighted match is tossed on to a carpet. The patient with brain failure lacks the ability to use past experience in order to anticipate future events. She throws the match away, heedless of the possible consequences.

INHIBITION

In infancy and in childhood, in privacy or in selected company, everyone has indulged in patterns of behaviour which are immediately gratifying but which are unacceptable in polite society. In adult life these patterns are suppressed, but the inhibitory mechanism can be weakened by drugs and alcohol and in brain failure. As a result offensive behaviour patterns may emerge. These are so different from normal behaviour as to constitute an apparent change of personality. They cause shock and horror to relatives and friends. Examples are swearing, carelessness in dress, refusal to wash, stripping off clothes, evacuating the bladder and bowels in the wrong places, sexual exposure, lewd suggestions and behaviour.

CONFABULATION

Confabulation means filling gaps in the memory by means of phrases, sentences, or stories designed to conceal the subject's ignorance from the questioner and from the subject herself. Confabulation is highly characteristic of the behaviour of patients with brain failure, especially of those who have a high level of education and who are articulate and remain so. The inventiveness shown by patients in confabulation is astounding. It is difficult to believe that people who can cover their tracks so ingeniously are nonetheless very much in need of doing so, because of the large gaps in their awareness. Confabulation may take the form of recounting lengthy stories, which appear highly plausible, but which are based on sheer fantasy or on recollection of distant events unrelated to the present situation. More common is the use of ambiguous phrases carefully selected to convey the impression that the question has been answered. A patient, when asked, 'Where have you been today?', may describe a long outing in great detail or may simply say coyly 'Wouldn't you like to know?'. This satisfies her as being an answer to the question, and gives her the impression that she has concealed the gap in her memory. If a patient is asked if she knows where she is, she indignantly asserts, 'Of course I do'; but if then asked again, 'Well, where are you?', she says, 'Here, of course', or, 'In this place', or a similar evasive answer. If the patient is asked, 'Who am I?' she is likely to reply, 'I know your face ... you're one of the people that are here', or more inventively, 'You are part of the administration of this place' or some such phrase.

Confabulators are not lying; they believe in the truth of their stories and are highly motivated to maintain this belief. The detection of confabulation is essential to the assessment of brain failure. It is easy for even the most experienced to be deceived, especially if the questioner does not introduce direct questions which cannot be brushed off. Caution is necessary also in the opposite sense, in that not all improbable stories are confabulation. For example a lady of 81 was thought to be confabulating when she said she lived with her mother, but this proved to be true: her mother was a fit 99-year-old!

DENIAL

Patients with brain failure explicitly deny allegations, the admission of which would amount to a confession of their intellectual disintegration. A patient who has been caught in the act of slipping a pair of urine-soaked knickers into a kitchen drawer, first denied indignantly that she had done anything of the sort, then insisted that this was her bedroom drawer, then said the knickers were perfectly clean, and finally that they were not her knickers anyway. Patients with brain failure also deny antisocial acts like prowling around the house during the night, stealing from other people, or swearing, and may do so both because they have forgotten having committed the 'offences' of which they are accused, and because they believe that this is not the sort of thing they would ever do.

PERSEVERATION

Perseveration is the repetition of the response to a previous stimulus. The severely brain-damaged patient, told to put out her tongue, does so. If she is then told to lift her hands she puts out her tongue again. In less severe cases of brain failure the patient defends herself against the demands of a new situation by employing behaviour patterns appropriate to an old one. A hospital patient got up and walked out of the ward at five o'clock every evening when he heard the siren in the nearby factory, because he was reproducing a behaviour pattern of his former working life.

FLUCTUATION

Fluctuation of intellectual energy and clarity occurs in normal people as well as in those with brain failure. At their best the latter can remember and think almost normally, while at their worst, especially in the early evening and in the small hours of the morning, they can be very confused and noisy. The unwary may be so impressed by the islands of lucidity that they fail to take the patient's brain failure seriously, and form an incorrect idea that the old person is 'having them on'.

Normal diurnal rhythms are altered in brain failure. Patients may be active and hungry in the middle of the night and drowsy and somnolent by day. They 'turn night into day', and their internal clocks are at variance with those of the rest of the world. This socially disruptive behaviour, which exhausts relatives, seems to be resistant to correction by hypnotic drugs.

An analogy

A rough analogy might be drawn between the brain and a lawyer's office which can be thought of as having four levels of activity represented by the counter, the office, the archives, and the cellar.

In the early stages of brain failure functional impairment is mainly of 'cross-counter transactions' i.e. the recognition of new items of information and immediate responses to them. At this stage the other functions are largely intact.

As the condition progresses access to the more complex background processes of organizing records of previous activities in the filing system and of relating them to the transactions taking place at the counter become affected.

The archives, that is the records of long past events, are intact until the late stages of the disease, but begin to obtrude upon and become confused with more recent and current activities.

The cellars contain rejected patterns of conduct from the long past, but in the late stages of the disease material from the cellars finds its way to the counter in error.

Assessment

In assessing the presence, duration, nature, and severity of brain failure the social worker depends on the observations of witnesses, the results of her own interview with the patient and her study of the patient's behaviour and environment. These forms of assessment are dealt with in detail in Chapter 10, pp.116–18. The social worker also depends to a limited extent on tests of mental function.

TESTS FOR BRAIN FAILURE

Formal testing should be approached with caution, since it is mainly a matter for the expert, and does not necessarily add a great deal to the information which a social worker can obtain from direct interview with the patient and relatives. Testing is artificial and threatening, and exposes the patient to embarrassment. If relatives are present they usually endeavour to 'help' the patient by providing answers and they may seem resentful of the tester. Neither the patient nor the relatives like to have the gaps in the patient's awareness exposed in public. This having been said, the following tests are nonetheless useful within limitations.

Newspaper test

Ask the patient to describe a picture in the newspaper, to read a paragraph of news, and to repeat the gist of what has been read. Performance of this test is influenced greatly by previous educational level, but it should be possible to detect a change from what might reasonably be expected of a mentally normal person comparable in other respects with the patient.

Digit reversal test

Give a three digit number to the patient, e.g. 892, ask her to repeat it and then to say the number backwards. If she succeeds try with a four digit number. Normal old people should have no difficulty with reversing a four digit number; patients with brain failure often fail with even a three digit number.

Set-test

Ask the patient to tell you how many different colours she can remember, and wait until she has exhausted her stock, begins to repeat herself, or to become anecdotal. Do not pump. Repeat for animals, fruits, and towns. Allow a maximum score of ten in each part of the test and thus a total maximum of forty. Many factors influence the score on this test, but it can be taken as a very rough guide that normal old people score 25 or better and those with brain failure score less than 15. The way in which the patient approaches the test is informative: many appear very confident at the beginning, produce a rush of three or four items, and then come to a sudden halt, offering confabulatory explanations such as 'I know dozens more'.

27

While these tests are of interest, mental function cannot be represented by a number on a scale.

Management

The principles of management of the patient with brain failure are to try to understand:

(i) why the patient behaves as she does;
(ii) what are the patient's needs;
(iii) why the relatives or other carers react as they do;
(iv) what are their needs;
(v) why you yourself react as you do;
(vi) what are your needs.

Commonly people get into difficulty by thinking of the patient as a rational being and reacting with irritation to her irrationality. When one is asked for the tenth time, 'What's for lunch?', it is natural to react by saying, 'That's the tenth time you've asked me.' But that only upsets the patient who doesn't remember the first nine times. To her it is still the first time and she still wants the answer.

Patients also react with unusual resentment and hostility to threatening questions or behaviour, and cannot understand that they have induced these. It is no use saying, 'Why did you do this?' to a person who has done something she would never have done in health. She did it because she has brain failure and because she does not want you to know that she has brain failure. Infinite patience, tolerance, humour, and unshockability are required.

Another source of difficulty is the resigned belief that nothing can be done to alter the abnormal behaviour. At the core of every patient with brain failure there is an interest, a skill, an activity that can still be undertaken successfully and that can give pleasure. Imagination and insight are required to find it. For example taking a group of hospital patients with severe brain failure on an outing to the local public house can be most instructive. Sitting at the bar with a pint of beer in their hands patients who have uttered not a single rational remark for months in the ward will sing songs, tell stories, make jokes, behave as they did when the brain was normal. Other patients derive similar gratification from visits to sporting events, shops, cinemas, parks, or church. Even when they may understand little of what is happening, they value and enjoy the experience of participation. The over-protected patient, confined to home or hospital, quickly becomes withdrawn and emotionally stunted, and is less likely to respond to activities. The carer has to think that she has a guest in her house who needs to be entertained. The programmes of Day Centres successfully incorporate this policy.

The problems of the carer are dealt with more fully in Chapter 11. In this chapter, we have given a mere outline of some of the principles of management. The manifestations of the disease are so many and so various that every carer could write a book about her experiences and about how she has learned to cope with them. At the heart of it all is the advice, so easy to give, so difficult to apply, to stop and think before reacting.

Summary

Many brain mechanisms are severely impaired in brain failure, and this influences the behaviour pattern of the patient, which is also affected by previous personality, environment, and the reaction of others. Analysis and explanation of patient behaviour can prevent unsuitable reactions, increase tolerance, and aid management.

4 OTHER MENTAL ILLNESS

The subject to be considered in this chapter comprises the more common mental illnesses in late life other than brain failure. These are often divided by psychiatrists into two main groups, the psychoses and the neuroses.

A *psychosis* is a major mental illness which has profound effects on the personality. The disease originates within the patient and is largely independent of external events.

In contrast a *neurosis* is thought of as an abnormal reaction to unfavourable external events. The basic personality remains intact and the psychiatric symptoms do not deprive the patient of insight.

The distinction between 'psychosis' and 'neurosis' is not always clear. Unfortunately the word 'neurotic' has entered lay language almost as a term of abuse. The 'neurotic' may be erroneously looked upon as a weak-willed self-indulgent person who needs to 'pull herself together'. To the psychiatrist neurosis is an illness which causes great distress, which may even be associated with excess mortality, and which requires careful assessment and compassionate treatment.

The affective disorders

Brain failure is predominantly an intellectual disturbance, although secondary emotional changes are common. The group of diseases known to psychiatrists as 'the affective disorders' are primarily disturbances of emotion – and intellectual changes, when they occur, are secondary.

The affective disorders are extremely common in the elderly, even more common than brain failure. But the conditions often

go unrecognized, or are looked upon as the unavoidable consequences of the deprivations of late life.

The affective disorders rarely occur in isolation – usually they
are accompanied by physical disease, by social loss and deprivation,
by brain failure, or by a combination of all three. For example,
a woman of 84 suffered from severe anxiety and bouts of depression.
She lived alone, had no relatives, had fallen repeatedly, and had lain
all night on the floor on two occasions. Furthermore the house next
door had been vandalized. She had apparently adequate reasons to
feel anxious and depressed, and yet these feelings were persistent
and pervasive and were judged to be abnormal. Her anxiety and
depression improved with drug treatment even though the adverse
physical and social factors persisted. It is possible, but unlikely,
that she might have recovered equally well if she had been rehoused
or given a course of physiotherapy and not received drugs. However, physical, social, and psychiatric factors are so intertwined in
the circumstances of many old people that an integrated approach
to treatment is the one most likely to yield favourable results.

Psychoses and neuroses may appear for the first time in old age.
More usually they occur first in earlier life and continue into old
age; or they may spontaneously remit or be treated successfully only
to reappear in later life.

DEPRESSION

Depression is the best known, but not necessarily the best understood, of the affective disorders. The term 'depression' is used in
three ways. First, it is used to describe understandable misery: the
expression of an emotion with which we can all identify when
circumstances go seriously wrong. For the old person this might
be bereavement, especially loss of a spouse; retirement; serious and
disabling physical illness, for example amputation of a leg; moving
from the family home into residential accommodation; children
leaving home. These are all associated with a feeling of loss.
Depression in this sense may also be associated with loss of self-
esteem, deteriorating health, inability to take part in social
activities, diminution of status, or decrease of spending power.
Such states are common in old age, and the resulting unhappiness
does not amount to illness.

Second, is the condition known as 'reactive depression' in which
a more definite and prolonged state of misery is accompanied by
inability to cope with the demands of everyday life. Although this

31

state of mind is precipitated by factors such as have been described, it persists with undue intensity and leads to inappropriate behaviour in dealing with problems. Recurrent stresses may cause repeated episodes of depression.

A third type is when severe feelings of depression occur apparently out of the blue, without precipitating cause. This is called 'endogenous' depression. Profound depression of mood is accompanied by retardation of thinking and physical activity. Vitality is lowered and this affects biological, physical, and psychological function.

Clinical features of endogenous depression in the elderly
The symptoms of endogenous depression include:

(i) loss of appetite;
(ii) loss of weight;
(iii) constipation, which may become a focus for hypochondriacal ideas;
(iv) disturbance of sleep, characteristically early morning waking; or waking repeatedly during the night with difficulty in getting back to sleep.

The depression is worst in the morning. There is general slowing of all motor activity. Speech is slow and monotonous, behaviour is sluggish, and the appearance is miserable. Hypochondriacal ideas are common. Physical complaints are exaggerated and cause undue concern to the patient, who may harbour delusional beliefs that she has cancer, that her bowels are blocked, that 'things are coming to an end', that bodily functions will no longer work. Symptoms may be located in the head, the stomach, or other organ of the body. They may have the character not so much of pain as of a feeling of discomfort, tension, or pressure.

Feelings of guilt and unworthiness are prominent. There is depreciation of self, which may amount to nihilistic delusion. An example is an elderly man who looked out of his window with gloomy foreboding, in the certain belief that the police were coming to collect him, because he had forsaken the front line in the First World War nearly sixty years before. Patients blame themselves for their condition and consider it a justifiable punishment. They lose interest and enthusiasm for reading, gardening, or any other hobby, and no longer even make spontaneous conversation.

Difficulty in concentration is experienced, due at least in part to preoccupation with gloomy thoughts. There is an apparent loss of memory and poor performance on mental tests. The apparent loss of memory must be distinguished from the loss of memory found in dementia (brain failure). The poor performance in depression is due to inattention, preoccupation, and retardation. The patient cannot attend to the matter in hand long enough to register the information, nor can she think and act fast enough to respond.

Loss of ability to feel emotion is common. Tolerance for noise is often reduced, so that conversation, television, or children's talk sound unduly loud and unpleasant. Loss of libido occurs. Commonly patients experience the feeling that life is not worth living, and a significant number commit suicide. Many patients are perplexed by their inability to identify a cause for the illness. One patient said, 'I don't know why I am letting everybody down so badly. I've got a good husband and two marvellous daughters. We have no money problems now that they are all grown up. I just cannot be with my grandchildren and yet I love them.'

OTHER VARIETIES OF DEPRESSION

'*Manic-depressive psychosis*'

This type of depression is cyclical. An attack may last for three to six months, followed by a complete remission, then by another attack many years later. Attacks of mania and depression may alternate in the same person with periods of health in between. There is a tendency with the passage of time for the intervals between attacks to shorten. There is also a grave risk of suicide.

Depressive stupor

In about 10 per cent of elderly depressives, the condition starts with a phase of 'clouding of consciousness', characterized by disorientation, fluctuating levels of attention, and loss of intellectual grasp. The risk of suicide at this time is particularly great. In depressive stupor the degree of retardation becomes so profound that physical activity and speech stop altogether. The patient sits mute and motionless, failing to eat and drink. Urgent treatment is essential.

Agitated depression

In agitated depression the patient is profoundly and often suicidally depressed with motor restlessness, over-activity, extravagant ideas of guilt and unworthiness, and nihilistic and hypochondriacal

33

delusions. The patient rushes about wringing her hands, and detailing past misdemeanours in an exaggerated way. Again, failure to institute urgent treatment would be negligent.

TREATMENT OF ENDOGENOUS DEPRESSION
The treatment of depression is just as effective in the elderly as in younger people, although the side effects may be rather more troublesome in the elderly. The two chief methods of medical treatment are anti-depressant drugs and electroconvulsive therapy. 80 per cent of patients with endogenous depression who are treated with adequate dosage of drugs are improved. It usually takes up to two weeks or longer before improvement begins.

Electroconvulsive therapy (ECT) is indicated for patients who are so severely ill that it would not be safe to wait for the beneficial action of anti-depressants, and for those who have not responded to drug treatment. Modern methods of giving ECT are safe and humane and cause little or no distress to the patient. Since a general anaesthetic is used the treatment is given only to patients who are fit for anaesthesia. There is loss of memory for the treatment and for a short period preceding it. In some old patients a period of confusion may follow the treatment. The risks and discomforts of ECT are very much less than are those of the untreated disease.

Home or hospital treatment
Severely depressed people normally need in-patient treatment. Many depressed people do not realize that they are ill, or alternatively believe that their symptoms are a rightful punishment. They therefore do not present for treatment, refuse treatment, or resist admission to hospital.

Explanation and persuasion by the social worker can be most helpful in these circumstances.

SUICIDE
The incidence of successful suicide increases with increasing age (although in late life the rate for attempted suicide diminishes) and at all ages is more common in males than in females (see *Table 2*). In England and Wales between 1960 and 1969 death rates for suicide fell from eleven to nine per 100,000 population. In men the drop was from fourteen to eleven and in women from nine to seven (World Health Organisation 1963, 1972).

Table 2   *Suicide*
*Average annual suicide rates per million of population, England and Wales,
1969–71 by age and sex.*

age	men	women
15–24	56	24
25–34	96	44
35–44	120	64
45–54	140	100
55–64	180	124
65–74	220	140
75–84	240	120

Source: Ross and Kreitman (1975).

Suicide is underrepresented, in official statistics, because Coroners are discouraged from bringing in this verdict unless they have evidence of suicidal intent. An unknown number of people recorded as having died accidentally have killed themselves.

All cases of overdose or other self-harming behaviour should be regarded as serious suicide attempts. Sainsbury (1968) found evidence of mental illness in 93 per cent of suicides, and in 70 per cent depression was considered to be present. Alcoholism was another major condition predisposing to suicide. 80 per cent of suicides had recently consulted their family doctors and 80 per cent had been prescribed psychotropic drugs.

Sainsbury (1968) found in his study of suicide in old people that 35 per cent had been suffering from physical illness, 39 per cent had been living alone, and 16 per cent had been recently bereaved. Many had previously admitted to experiencing suicidal ideas, or had made previous attempts at suicide. Lack of occupation contributed to an increased likelihood of suicide, while those with a religious faith were less likely to kill themselves. The tone of many suicide notes is eloquent of the feeling of worthlessness and being a burden. An old person who lives on her own and who becomes depressed is at real risk of suicide; the risk can be reduced by social action.

MANIA

The term 'mania' is used by psychiatrists to describe a condition in which patients become extremely active and excited and may constitute a danger to themselves and others. Milder manifestations of this condition are often called 'hypomania', but this term will not be used in this book. We do not, after all, talk about 'hypo-depression' with reference to minor degrees of depression. Using two names for what is essentially the same condition carries the danger of confusing the issue.

Depression and mania may occur as different episodes of illness in the same patient, but mania is much less common than depression. It occurs in about 5 to 10 per cent of cases of affective disorder in the elderly. Half of these cases are recurrent attacks in patients who suffered from manic-depressive psychosis at a younger age, and the other half are first attacks.

Characteristically this condition starts suddenly with excessive talkativeness, flight of ideas, and extreme overactivity. The mood may be unreasonably cheerful, or else display the frustrated irritability of a person whose energies are continually being denied expression. Commonly the mood state is preceded by depression, which may not come to professional attention or cause concern.

Mania greatly upsets family routine. The patient may carry out bizarre and grandiose schemes. One patient made compost out of old mattresses and buried them all over his garden. Another patient felt that his wife should not have to traverse the yard to reach the outdoor lavatory, so he knocked a hole in the brickwork between the kitchen and the lavatory, meaning to put a new door in its place – but before doing so he decided to rewire the house and started to pull the old wiring out.

The 'flight of ideas' is reflected in the patient's talk, which proceeds from idea to idea, with logical links between statements, but without these being explained, and without a clear goal in the conversation. The patient is highly distractible. Puns, jokes, and 'clang associations' (association between words of similar sound, but of different meaning) are common. The patient may have grandiose or persecutory delusions.

Treatment of mania

Mania is an indication for admission to hospital using, if necessary, the powers of the Mental Health Act, 1959. The patient may exhaust herself by overactivity, lack of sleep, and rejection of food.

She may indulge in behaviour that is dangerous to herself or to others. The high risk of serious harm may not be obvious, because of the cheerfulness and apparent benevolence of the patient. In hospital, with skilful psychiatric nursing and the use of major tranquillizing drugs, treatment is usually satisfactory, with a return to normal mood in a few weeks. Occasionally mania becomes chronic and resistant to treatment. The introduction of new drugs has greatly improved the management of manic-depressive psychosis, and reduced the likelihood of recurrence. The treatment is complex and close supervision is necessary.

SCHIZOPHRENIA AND PARANOID STATES

Schizophrenia in the elderly comprises first, patients who had schizophrenic illnesses at an earlier age, and who have residual defect; and second, those developing schizophrenia or a schizo-phrenia-like illness for the first time in old age.

There is a large and ageing population of people who have been in hospital with schizophrenia for many years and who have severe residual symptoms. Some of these patients may now be living at home or in hostels or lodgings. They may have some delusions and hallucinations, but the major part of their symptomatology is 'negative': blunting or flattening of affect and lack of volition. They are often so inert that they can survive outside hospital only with the support of others, for example a parent. When they lose their social support or develop physical illness, they can no longer cope and require social work help, or admission to hospital, or both.

Schizophrenia starting *de novo* in the elderly has similarities to and differences from the condition in younger age groups. The peak age for onset of schizophrenia is between 15 and 25 for males, and 10 years later for females. However, there is a subsidiary peak over the age of 75. Kay (1963) has pointed out that 4 per cent of all schizophrenic illnesses in males and 14 per cent in females occur after the age of 65.

Clinical features of schizophrenia

Schizophrenia is a serious mental illness characterized by a fundamental disturbance of the whole person, so that feelings are altered in terms of individuality, uniqueness, and self-direction. The clinical picture is very variable. A characteristic form in old age is the condition called *paraphrenia*, in which there are delusions, hallucinations, and disorders of thought. The delusions of schizophrenia are about the patient herself. They may be persecutory, grandiose, sexual, hypochondriacal, or religious. An example of a paraphrenic delusion was an isolated elderly spinster with beliefs that men were trying to enter her home at night and interfering with her sexually. Delusions may become systematized; the logical developments of the initially false 'belief spread into all areas of life, so that bizarre behaviour and elaborate precautions become necessary.

The schizophrenic patient also commonly suffers auditory hallucinations such as hearing voices, which express the patient's own thoughts aloud, comment on her actions, and argue with other disembodied voices about her. The voice is heard clearly and is unlike the internal voice of conscience. Hallucinations of touch, taste, and smell may also occur. The patient has great difficulty in describing her experiences. Sometimes she creates new words and new meanings of words to fill this deficiency. Other features of schizophrenia include disorders of thought, inconsistent thinking, blunting of emotion, inappropriate laughter, depression, lack of volition, and abnormal stereotyped movements.

Schizophrenics are characteristically isolated and remote, without close human contacts or friends, neglectful, inclined to live as taciturn odd recluses. Hearing loss and blindness may predispose to this condition. The prognosis is very variable.

Treatment of schizophrenia

A proportion of patients respond to anti-psychotic drugs, and are able to live out of hospital. They may lose their symptoms altogether. The 'active' symptoms such as delusions and hallucinations respond better to treatment than the 'passive' symptoms such as flattening of affect and lack of volition. When the relatives are not critical of the patient's behaviour, the likelihood of relapse is lower. Maintenance therapy with anti-psychotic drugs is required.

The social worker can help neighbours to understand the patient's bizarre behaviour, and to tolerate her eccentricities, and thereby help her to survive outside hospital.

Psychotherapy has not improved the lot of most schizophrenics but has a place in helping those who have been treated for acute symptoms to come to terms with their condition. Behavioural methods of treatment have been used; for example operant conditioning, using a token economy, has had some success in improving the way in which chronic institutionalized schizophrenic patients function.

PARANOIA

There is discussion amongst psychiatrists concerning the existence of a third psychosis that does not precisely conform to either schizophrenia or manic depressive psychosis but has some features of both. In the elderly, paranoia occupies this intermediate state. Patients have a single dominating delusion which becomes elaborated to affect all areas of their thinking but they do not have hallucinations or any disorganization of personality. Delusions of persecution and sexual delusions are common. On all other topics of conversation, the patient may reveal nothing unusual. She may show marked abnormality of mood, depression, and suspiciousness. These delusions are often completely resistant to treatment and are retained indefinitely. However, major tranquillizers may produce some improvement in some cases.

Neuroses

Neurosis is often overlooked as a cause of distress in old people and of poor relationships with those around them. In the Newcastle survey (Kay, Beamish, and Roth 1964) neurosis was the most common mental disorder in old age. The most common symptoms in the elderly neurotic are misery, tension, anxiety, loss of self-esteem and hypochondriasis. Phobic, obsessional, and sensitive symptoms occur less commonly.

Neurosis is a type of behaviour or a way of life that is inappropriate in solving problems so that failure to cope becomes habitual. It is common at all ages. A person who has responded neurotically when young is likely to do so in later life. Others may demonstrate neurotic reactions for the first time late in life, on first exposure to such stresses as loss of employment, status, relatives, or health.

Physical illness in later life may sap confidence and self-esteem, leaving the victims less able to relate to their fellows on an equal footing, and this inability can lead to withdrawal from life and despondent and anxious feelings.

MANAGEMENT OF NEUROSIS

The aim of treatment is to help the patient to manage her affairs in a more satisfactory way and to make sensible decisions. If she

39

is physically incapacitated and cannot live on her own, she may need help in deciding where to live and with whom. One neurotic patient insisted on living with the daughter she had always got on badly with, as a sort of punishment for both of them. While formal psychotherapy is not generally appropriate in old age, patients can be helped to gain insight. Drugs may be useful in the treatment of anxiety, tension, and insomnia. The combination of social and psychological approaches helps to improve self-esteem.

Alcoholism and drug dependence

These are not common in old age. Alcoholism carries a high mortality rate and so some alcoholics die before becoming old. In others alcohol produces irreparable brain damage so that they suffer from chronic brain failure. Still others overcome their addiction with or without treatment.

A small number of old people become alcoholic for the first time in later life. They are not infrequently secretive in their drinking habits. Some old people seem remarkably unaffected by large quantities of alcohol, but others show emotional lability, forgetfulness, confabulation, and physical deterioration. The alert social worker may hit upon the diagnosis by detecting the 'empties' or when discussing income and expenditure with a client.

Alcoholism is a treatable condition, but this depends on the co-operation and the will of the patient.

DRUG DEPENDENCE

Dependence on a drug may be because the drug acts to cause a pleasant state of mind; or because the person is dependent on the idea of being treated; or because the drug is treating the symptoms of the illness which return when the drug is stopped.

Old people may be physically dependent on barbiturates, or more rarely on analgesic drugs (such as pethidine and morphine). Emotional dependence is experienced especially with hypnotic and anxiolytic drugs.

Recognition of dependence does not automatically lead to withdrawal of the drug. The question should be asked, especially for old and infirm people, which course of action offers the best quality of life, removing or continuing the medication?

Some forensic aspects of mental disorder in old age

Some forms of unacceptable behaviour are associated with mental illness. Other issues of forensic importance such as the Mental Health Act, testamentary capacity and clinical responsibility are discussed elsewhere. (See Appendix 1, pp.167–8; Appendix 2, pp.169–70; pp.54–6.) Disturbed old people may indulge in reprehensible behaviour because they do not know what they are doing, or do not appreciate the suffering caused by their actions.

Physical violence rarely results from mental illness. In depression, feelings of guilt and violence are commonly directed against the self, but occasionally violence is turned against property or other people. Rarely a depressed person commits homicide within the family then suicide. A person suffering from mania may, rarely, if frustrated in his intentions, commit violent acts arbitrarily and without malice. Sometimes violence occurs in association with schizophrenia, especially of catatonic type. It may also result from the patient's psychotic experience – he breaks his neighbour's door down because he believes she has been trapped there by Marxists. Crimes involving physical violence are commonly associated with alcohol intoxication and alcoholism.

Unacceptable sexual behaviour occurs occasionally amongst the elderly mentally infirm. Deviant tendencies which have been prevented from manifesting themselves over the years gain expression for the first time, as a consequence of brain damage. Paedophilia may occur when sexual advances are made to children of either sex. Exhibitionism is not uncommon amongst old men, who are usually not charged with this offence. Homosexual or incestuous approaches may be made for the first time.

Mental illness, commonly depression, is a factor in some of those charged with theft and shoplifting. Shoplifting of this kind may be a way of gaining attention, of punishing the relative, or of seeking punishment for imagined misdeeds.

It is sometimes difficult to know whether a fire started by an old person was deliberate and malicious, or was merely due to the mistaken belief that she was making a fire in an appropriate place. Investigation of crimes necessitates a careful psychiatric history and examination and a social report, involving appraisal of such social support as is available and consideration of ways of improving it.

Summary

A wide range of psychiatric disorders occur in the elderly. These comprise very much the same psychiatric conditions as are familiar in younger patients, but their manifestations in old age may differ and they may be difficult to distinguish one from another, especially when they are accompanied, as they often are, by physical illness. Abnormal behaviour in old people should never be regarded as normal simply because the people are old, nor is all of it due to dementia. Expert psychiatric help is necessary as a prerequisite to social intervention.

5 NORMAL AND ABNORMAL PERSONALITY

Definition of personality

By personality we understand broadly the sum total of personal attributes. The forces which shape personality have their greatest influence in early life. William James went so far as to say that 'In most of us, by the age of 30, the character is set like plaster, and will never soften again'. Some psychologists believe that certain people continue to develop throughout life, rather as an old wine matures, and that other less well-balanced personalities can adjust to and even enjoy the ageing process. Other psychologists believe that personality changes in late life because of altered life experience or as a result of neurophysiological changes or disease. D. B. Bromley (1974) gives a well-documented, extended account of personality, especially of the changes through middle age into old age. Older people have to adapt to reduction in strength, physical endurance, metabolism, and memory. An increasing number of them come to prefer undemanding physical activities and inter-action within small groups, and to dislike competition and to prefer solitude. They seek caution, convention, and conformity. They show lessened self-confidence, less inclination to spend time in the company of others, and less close personal relationships.

The narrowing of interests, restriction of activities, increased rigidity, and difficulties in decision making which are commonly observed in very old people could be the result of deterioration of neurological mechanisms which serve short-term storage of infor-mation and learning. Decline in these functions, combined with lessened drive and lessened personal motivation, may be respon-sible for some abnormal behaviour. Not all elderly people are equally handicapped by this loss of vigour. Some appear to retain their interests and faculties intact or nearly intact, until they die.

Psychological theories of ageing

According to the *activity theory*, which is particularly applicable to 'younger' old people, the healthy aged have the same psychological needs as the middle-aged. Withdrawal from life is against their inclinations, and is forced upon them by society which compels early retirement and which reduces natural opportunities for social intercourse. Successful ageing involves continuing active engagement in social roles, with the quest for substitutes for activities which can no longer be pursued, and with resistance to shrinkage of social contacts. (This view is expressed, rather wordily, in Blau (1973) and well summarized in Hendricks and Hendricks (1977).)

Disengagement theory was set out by Cumming and Henry (1961). It has been the focus for innumerable articles since, agreeing or disagreeing with more or less fury. This theory of ageing, more applicable to the very old, sees old age as the period when, for the first time in the life-cycle, there is no new horizon to look forward to with new responsibilities and challenges. Activities and social interaction which were characteristic of middle age become curtailed. People become increasingly preoccupied with themselves and are less involved with the outside world. This is a withdrawal of the individual from society rather than of society from the individual. The person who ages successfully in this sense achieves a new equilibrium, with a greater distance from those around him and with fewer social interactions. Apparent apathy may merely be successful disengagement.

Personality types and their adjustment to ageing

A study of men on both sides of retirement by Reichard and her colleagues (1962) led to the following analysis of personality types:

(i) *The mature* These are well-integrated men with some self-awareness, who are able to enjoy life, to make warm personal relations, and to assume family responsibilities. They value retirement for the chance to spend more time with family and friends and to develop personal interests. They have constructive, optimistic, future-oriented attitudes towards the process of ageing.

(ii) *The rocking-chair men* These tend to lean on others for material and emotional support. They are unambitious, and are happy to take things easy. They are placid and dependent. They are glad to retire and to detach themselves from earlier responsibilities.

(iii) *The armoured men* These are over-controlled, conventional, and compulsively active men. They seek part-time employment after retirement, or organize a daily schedule of activities. People of this type adjust well to ageing but fail to savour it. Their strategy is defensive.

(iv) *The angry men* They are constantly on the lookout for hostility. They are intolerant of frustration and have a pessimistic attitude to life. They tend to put the blame for their own failures on other people or on their bad circumstances. They defend themselves against old age by a compulsion to remain active. They see retirement as the beginning of the end. They see no good in old age and fear death.

(v) *The self-haters* These men turn their hostility upon themselves. They have a low opinion of themselves, are depressed, and flaunt their own miseries and shortcomings. They have little warmth or affection for their wives or families. They look back on their past with regret and self-recrimination, and forward to death as a merciful release from an unsatisfactory existence.

This analysis demonstrates that old age has its psychological gains as well as its losses. The barriers to good adjustment appear to lie in the personality itself rather than in social circumstances and 'mature' individuals are not the only ones who savour old age.

Personality disorders

Personality disorder is not a disease; it is the product of unfortunate life experiences, such as deprivation, loss, conflict, and failure. Abnormal personality characteristics may be exaggerated in late life. The following types of abnormal personality are recognized:

(i) *Paranoid personality* People with paranoid personality are highly suspicious. They believe that others are taking notice of them in an unpleasant and derogatory way. The *passive* type faces the world from a position of submission and humiliation, knowing that whatever happens will be for the worst. When she meets new people she assumes that they will not like her, and she fears that her friends will take advantage

45

of her. The *active* type is more aggressive and less accepting. She is quarrelsome and litigious and may go to elaborate lengths to defend her rights and to redress what she considers to be injustice. In old age both types of paranoid personality become accentuated. The active type becomes more hostile and cantankerous; the passive more suspicious and vulnerable. Within the family or in the residential home both types cause difficulty in personal relationships.

(ii) *The affective personality* The person with a depressive personality is persistently anxious, gloomy, depressed, and miserable. She sits in the corner of a room doing nothing, and is reluctant to join with others in activities. The cyclothymic personality shows marked fluctuations of moods. One day she is optimistic, energetic, garrulous, and full of plans and ideas; the next she is gloomy and taciturn.

(iii) *The schizoid personality* People of this type are disinclined to mix with others and appear withdrawn and aloof. Their apparent loneliness is not relieved by admission to a home.

(iv) *The explosive personality* These people become irritable, angry, or violent with quite slight provocation. They exploit other people's fear of them to gain their own ends. They are unpopular and disruptive.

(v) *The obsessive compulsive personality* Members of this group harbour feelings of insecurity and meticulous conscientiousness. They are very sensitive to the views of others. They are shy and awkward in company and have difficulty in expressing emotion. They carry out duties precisely and with attention to detail. They are tidy and houseproud to a fault. They are conformist in behaviour and rigid in their social and moral attitudes. They are indecisive and they agonize about choices. They accept the strictures of others without question. They find it difficult to initiate or to complete an activity. Their over-conscientiousness makes them useful in an organization but difficult to live with. Their rigid views may cause friction, particularly if the family group includes adolescents. They are susceptible to depressive breakdown in old age.

(vi) *Hysterical personality* People of this type rapidly form excellent but superficial relationships with new acquaintances. They have difficulty in sustaining close long-term mutually rewarding relationships. They are labile in their mood and emotions. They crave attention and affection from others. They tend to be histrionic and over-dramatic, and they are prime manipulators in their relationships with others. They attempt to control and manipulate the family. They express fear of rejection and make their children feel guilty. Hysterical personalities retain control and dominance, but cause distress and mistrust. In a residential home they at first appear charming and sociable, but soon cause disharmony, because of undue demands for love and attention.

(vii) *Asthenic personality* These are inadequate people who lack mental energy and adaptability and who cannot cope with the stresses and demands of life. In old age their dependent and passive attitudes may become advantageous particularly if they enter a residential home.

(viii) *Antisocial personality* These people are oblivious of others. They lack conscience and human sympathy, and are cruel, callous, and aggressive. In both the family and in an institutional setting their actions are very disruptive.

(ix) *Anxious personality* Anxiety increases with age, and old people with an anxious personality may fear falling, becoming incontinent, or becoming dependent, but they rarely fear death. Anxiety may manifest itself by sweating, palpitations, tremor, exaggerated behaviour, and restlessness. In a residential home anxiety may lead to excessive demands to be toiletted and to preoccupation with excretion.

MANAGEMENT

Abnormal personality is not a mental illness and does not lend itself to treatment, although some of the manifestations of anxiety and depression are treatable. The most helpful approach is to understand that old people who suffer from stress and frustration because of physical and mental limitations become over-anxious, irritable, even violent. It is no use expecting the schizoid personality to be a good mixer. The cyclothymic personality with her fluctuations in mood should be given outlets for activity when she has a surge of energy. She may also need to be cheered when she is feeling depressed. The obsessional personality feels better if she is kept busy and is reassured by being asked to be responsible for little jobs such as watering the plants or collecting newspaper money. In group situations incompatible personalities should be kept apart. Those who share old people's lives and who understand their difficulties should try to arrange situations so as to reduce frustration and limit unacceptable behaviour.

Summary

Human personality presents in an infinite variety of forms and is moulded by the experiences of life. Nonetheless it is possible to make out, if rather dimly, certain personality 'types' and certain patterns of reaction to the vicissitudes of late life. The strange behaviour of the abnormal personality is not amenable to psychiatric or medical treatment, and the best that one can do is to try to understand and to tolerate.

6 THE NATIONAL HEALTH SERVICE AND THE ELDERLY MENTALLY INFIRM

This chapter deals with the care of the mentally infirm by the primary care, geriatric, and psychiatric services. The roles of social service departments and the voluntary organizations will be considered in a subsequent chapter.

Primary care

In the British National Health Service the general practitioner is responsible for the medical care of people of all ages who are registered with him while they are living in their own homes. He is the agent through whom hospital and specialist care and advice are provided. Every action of a hospital doctor or social worker which has any bearing on the patient's medical state requires the knowledge and consent of the general practitioner. Good communication between the general practitioner, the hospital, and the social service staff is essential for an effective service. Communication is complex and will be dealt with more fully in Chapter 10.

THE GENERAL PRACTICE REVOLUTION

Major changes in the organization of general practice took place in the United Kingdom in the late 1960s. Many single-handed general practitioners, working from lock-up premises and providing a twenty-four hours a day, seven-days a week service of consultation, home visiting, and emergency care, were superseded by the 'primary care team'. The majority of practitioners now work in groups from purpose-built health centres or from adapted premises, assisted by receptionists and secretaries, and they have practice nurses, community nurses, and health visitors working closely with them. Their premises are open all day, their patients are seen by appointment only, and home visits are much reduced. A rota system takes care of evening and weekend calls, or a locum service is employed. These changes provide more agreeable conditions for the doctor and better service for most patients, especially for the young and those with cars and telephones.

Effects on the elderly mentally infirm
Some aspects of reorganized general practice are potentially valuable for the elderly with mental illness. The attachment of community nurses and health visitors to the practice, and the availability of a register of patients by age and sex, give to the practitioner the opportunity of organizing surveillance for the identification of early manifestations of mental illness and for the taking of preventive action. At meetings of the practice team information from the community nurse and health visitor about isolated old people can be brought to the attention of the doctor. However, relatively few practices have introduced screening. Others might like to do so, but the quantity of help available from community nurses and health visitors, and the many other demands on their services, limit the feasibility. The new system of care also has two disadvantages for the elderly, particularly those who lack telephones and motor cars, of increased distance from the practice and difficulty in making contact. On balance the revolution in general practice has not conferred impressive advantages on the elderly with mental infirmity.

Hospital services for old people
Patients of all ages are admitted to general medical, surgical, psychiatric, and specialist wards in National Health Service hospitals. Specialized facilities for some elderly are available in departments of geriatric medicine, and in psychogeriatric units.

DEPARTMENTS OF GERIATRIC MEDICINE
Departments of geriatric medicine have developed more extensively and more distinctively in the United Kingdom than in most other countries. There is however continuing debate about their role, and about whether it is necessary and desirable for special facilities to be created for the elderly. This subject is best understood historically.

History

In the nineteenth century the physically infirm elderly were accommodated, along with many other groups of deprived people, in workhouses and in infirmaries for the chronic sick and incurable. The medical advances of the first half of the twentieth century largely passed these people by. When the National Health Service was introduced in 1948 these institutions came under scrutiny and were found to be grossly unsatisfactory. (See Thompson (1949) for a vivid description of the condition of patients in the hospital blocks of former Poor Law institutions.) Doctors were appointed to develop the services for the underprivileged elderly in substandard buildings. They succeeded in improving standards of care and in demonstrating that physical and mental deterioration, far from being the natural lot of old people, were all too often the consequence of undiagnosed and untreated illness. Rehabilitation and medical treatment restored health and independence to those for whom hope had been abandoned. Geriatric medicine is anxious to get away from the 'workhouse' image of the speciality and to acquire accommodation, facilities, skills, and staff equivalent to those provided in general medical wards.

Modern departments of geriatric medicine

The modern department of geriatric medicine is under the direction of two or more consultant physicians, well trained in general medicine, and with additional knowledge of and interest in the medical, psychiatric, rehabilitation, and social aspects of disease in the elderly. They are supported by adequate junior medical staff. A proportion of the beds of the department are located in general hospitals, where the geriatric physicians enjoy the same access to diagnostic and treatment facilities as do their colleagues in general medicine. The geriatric physician accepts a commitment to comprehensive assessment and continuous management of every aspect of his patient's problem. To assist him he has the services of hospital and community nurses, physiotherapists, occupational therapists, speech therapists, social workers, and administrators; and he welds these into a team who devote their skills to the declared objectives of comprehensive service and effective use of well-defined resources.

Unhappily this description applies to only a proportion of departments of geriatric medicine. In many parts of the country resources fall far below what is required. Consultants may have to work single-handed with little support from junior staff. The department's beds may be scattered through a number of hospitals, distant from one another and from the community which they serve, and lacking in modern diagnostic facilities and in the stimulus of colleagues. Diagnostic facilities may be hard to come by. Ancillary staff and community services may be insufficient. In these circumstances the department has difficulty in meeting the demands upon it and in providing an effective service for its potential clients.

Resources of departments of geriatric medicine

The National Health Service aims to provide geriatric beds at a rate of 10 beds per 1,000 of population aged 65 and over. The national average figure (1977) is a little below this. This means that in a district with a population of 250,000, 12·5 per cent of whom are aged 65 and over, the department of geriatric medicine should have 300 beds. At least 30 per cent of these should be in a general hospital, the remainder being either in community hospitals (few of which have as yet been provided) or in a variety of more or less makeshift settings which include former tuberculosis, infectious disease and maternity hospitals, local cottage hospitals, small children's units, and former convalescent homes. Many departments are still based on converted workhouse buildings.

Day hospital places are provided at a rate of 2 places per 1,000 persons aged 65 and over, i.e. about 60 places in every district. These are preferably distributed over two or more sites to facilitate travel and to avoid having large groups of patients.

In a district geriatric service there should be two consultant physicians in geriatric medicine with supporting medical staff. The junior staff in departments in general hospitals should participate in teaching programmes.

Day hospital

Most day hospitals are purpose-built: some are in adapted premises, e.g. disused wards, chapels, or gymnasia. They should be located in the general hospital where they can be used both by in-patients and by day-patients, and where there is access for both groups to diagnostic and rehabilitation services. Some are located apart from the general hospital, but nearer to the patient's homes.

Day hospitals usually operate on five days a week. Generally patients arrive between 9 and 11 o'clock in the morning and depart between 2 and 5 o'clock in the afternoon. Unless they can be brought to the day hospital by private transport or hospital car they are dependent on the ambulance service, and may have to endure a long journey to and from the day hospital. Activities in the day hospital include medical assessment and diagnosis, physical rehabilitation, practice in the activities of daily living, art and craft work, games, entertainment, and social interaction. A meal is provided and some day hospitals offer in addition chiropody, bathing, hair care, visual and auditory assessment, dietary advice, and social counselling. The patient's attendance at day hospital also offers relief to caring relatives.

CRITERIA FOR REFERRAL TO GERIATRIC SERVICE
Patients are referred to a geriatric service on the basis of location, age, and the nature of the medical problem.

Location
Most geriatric services have defined catchment areas, and deal only with elderly patients whose home address is within the catchment area. This catchment area should be co-terminous with the boundaries of the National Health Service administrative health district and with the Social Services Area, as well as with the catchment areas for acute, psychiatric, and other services. This cannot always be realized. Because of the erratic distribution of hospital beds old people may be in the catchment area of the geriatric service of one hospital and of the psychiatric service of another hospital; while the catchment area of one geriatric service may relate to two, three, or more Social Services Areas and one or two health districts. A patient living on one side of the street may be sent to one hospital, and one living on the opposite side to a different hospital. These problems are annoying. However, the alternative of having no catchment areas would take us back to the past when sometimes no hospital would accept responsibility for an elderly patient, particularly one with mental disturbance. The definition of strict catchment areas, absurd though it must sometimes seem, has two clear advantages for patients: it defines a responsible service; and it ensures a reasonably even distribution of limited resources.

The rules about catchment areas are worked out in each district, and social workers should understand how their local system operates. For example, what happens if a patient whose home address is in the catchment area of one service goes to stay with a

Care of the Elderly Mentally Infirm

daughter whose home is in the area of another service, and becomes ill while there, necessitating possible admission? There is usually more flexibility about emergency admissions than there is about subsequent transfer to continuing care accommodation.

Age
Some departments of geriatric medicine accept patients only if they are above a defined minimum age, usually 60 or 65. Others admit younger patients who require the special facilities of the department, for example those with strokes requiring intensive rehabilitation. Most departments are reluctant to admit young patients with chronic disability, for example the brain-damaged victims of road accidents or patients with multiple sclerosis; indeed the Disabled Persons Act of 1959 discouraged them from so doing. Patients with mental illness are not always acceptable to geriatric departments, even if physical disease co-exists.

Some departments of geriatric medicine, especially those with a high proportion of their beds in general hospitals, elect to take all patients, other than those with surgical or psychiatric illness, who are above a certain age, usually 75, sometimes 65. These departments resemble general medical units, with a high proportion of emergency and short-term cases. Departments of this nature may experience particular difficulty in admitting elderly patients with mental illness.

Diagnosis
Multiple illness is common in the elderly and the exact diagnosis is not always known at the stage of referral. Difficulties may arise in deciding whether people are most suitably admitted to geriatric, medical, psychiatric, or social service units.
Geriatrics and general medicine. Except where age criteria are applied, the differentiation of 'geriatric' from 'medical' cases is imprecise. There is a lingering tendency to think of the 'geriatric' case as being less 'acute' than the 'medical' case. Most geriatricians however are anxious and willing to admit elderly patients who are acutely ill, provided they and their nursing staff can meet the patient's demands for intensive medical and nursing care.
Geriatric units and psychiatric units. There is a major source of difficulty here, since, while no doctor believes that there are such things as 'mindless bodies' and 'bodyless minds' (see Parnell 1968) there is nonetheless some polarization of function and resources between geriatric and psychiatric units, and some reluctance of

54

each type of department to accept certain patients with mixed disability. After a much-publicized but subsequently refuted paper,* the impression was gained in government circles that it was dangerous for patients with predominantly mental illness to be admitted to geriatric units and for those with predominantly physical illness to be admitted to psychiatric units. The Department of Health (1971a) then gave guidance in a document, *Services for Mental Illness Related to Old Age* (HM (72) 71), which defined the relative responsibilities of geriatric, psychiatric, and social service units for the elderly mentally infirm. The appendix to that document sets out guidelines for hospital services for mental illness related to old age. These read as follows:

1. Elderly patients who have grown old in hospitals for mentally ill.	Number diminishing. New accommodation not needed, but improved conditions.
2. Elderly patients with functional mental illness.	Service requirements contained within the guideline provision of 0·5 beds and 0·65 day places per 1,000 total population suggested for adult mental illness in HM (71) 97.
3. Elderly persons with mild dementia but not suffering from other significant physical disease or illness.	It is envisaged that persons in this group will be cared for at home or in local authority residential accommodation.
4. Elderly patients with severe dementia but not suffering from other significant physical disease or illness.	2·5 to 3 beds plus 2 to 3 day places per 1,000 population aged 65 and over. This is additional to the scale of provision suggested for adult mental illness in HM (71) 97.
5. Elderly patients with dementia, whether mild or severe, and also suffering from other significant physical disease or illness.	Service requirements contained within the recommended planning guideline of 10 beds and 2 day places per 1,000 population aged 65 and over for geriatric services.

* The original is by Kidd (1962). It was largely refuted by, amongst others, Mezey, Hodkinson, and Evans (1968).

6. Elderly patients requiring joint geriatric/psychiatric assessment.

10 to 20 beds per quarter million total population as suggested in HM (70) 11. Normally to be sited in the geriatric department of the district general hospital.

This attempt to define relative responsibilities has proved helpful, but the definitions allowed for contradictory interpretations. There should be no difficulty about the physically ill being admitted to a geriatric unit, even if they have some degree of mental disturbance; or about the mentally ill being admitted to a psychiatric unit, provided they have no physical illness. A geriatric case does not become a psychiatric one merely because there are no available geriatric beds and vice versa. There remains the difficulty about cases with mixed physical and mental disability. So long as the patient has a significant physical illness, the geriatric service will generally cope with concomitant mental disturbance. Psychiatric departments deal with much physical disability, including incontinence, amongst their hospital population. The greatest difficulty arises with patients who have a tendency to wander. Geriatric departments are reluctant to take them, because they require so much nursing time and observation. Psychiatric wards are reluctant for the same reason, and because they do not wish to have to lock wards after abandoning that policy. Neither side wishes to destroy the patient's mobility, and much less the personality by the administration in large doses of tranquillizing drugs. The provision of a joint psychogeriatric assessment unit (see below), fails to solve the problem, which is one of management rather than of assessment.

Geriatric units and Social Service Departments
The relative responsibility of these two departments, as defined in HM 72 (71), takes little account of the ways in which the functional state can be altered by investigation and treatment. Many patients given help by Social Service Departments might be the better for a preliminary period of investigation and treatment in a geriatric unit. Proper placement of the mentally disturbed elderly occurs when the resources are reasonably adequate and people from the different services know one another personally, appreciate each other's difficulties and make personal contacts when they are in difficulty. Failure of management may occur when resources are

very inadequate, policies are applied inflexibly, and communication is by correspondence or by committee.

Admission policy

There are three main sources of admission of elderly patients to departments of geriatric medicine:

(i) Medical emergencies, i.e. old people who have become ill suddenly and who are likely to die or to recover quickly. They are sent in by the emergency bed service, from the hospital casualty department, or preferably by direct 'phone call from the general practitioner.

(ii) Old people at home or in residential homes with deterioration in physical, medical, and social competence of known or undetermined cause, requiring assessment and treatment or relief of carers. These patients are usually assessed before admission by the consultant geriatrician, either at home or at an out-patient or day hospital clinic.

(iii) Elderly patients in general, medical, surgical, psychiatric, or specialist hospital wards who are thought to need continuing care or rehabilitation in the geriatric service.

Departments of geriatric medicine differ in the emphasis which they place on these types of referral. Well-staffed departments try to help the first group, thereby achieving a high turnover, making beds available for other emergency admissions, and dispensing with a waiting list. Departments with limited resources receive fewer referrals for the first group and seldom have beds available in emergency. They tend to fill up with the second and third groups and to acquire a long waiting list. Every variation between these extremes can be found. The annual turnover rate of the unit, i.e. the number of patients treated per bed per annum, ranges from less than two to over ten.

Internal organization

Many departments of geriatric medicine divide their facilities into admission, rehabilitation, and continuing care areas, but others treat patients to completion in the wards to which they were first admitted. Almost all have in addition out-patient clinics and day hospitals. Most departments hold multi-disciplinary case conferences to assess the progress of in-patients and day patients and to plan discharges.

Social workers both from hospital and from area teams can help greatly at these conferences.

Psychiatric service

Psychiatry in the United Kingdom was formerly based on mental hospitals, most of which were constructed in the nineteenth century, distant from the communities which they served. Recently psychiatric departments have been established in many general hospitals, and the number of beds in mental hospitals has been reduced. There was at one time an expectation that the greatly improved treatment of chronic psychotic illness in younger people might make it possible for the mental hospitals eventually to be closed. This has not proved generally possible. There is good co-operation in some districts between general hospital psychiatric units and the mental hospital, but in other districts there is conflict of roles. Elderly patients are usually cared for in mental hospitals.

PSYCHOGERIATRICS

A recent innovation in the United Kingdom has been the emergence of interest in the psychiatry of old age. This is reflected in the formation of a section for the psychiatry of old age within the Royal College of Psychiatrists. This section supports the establishment of consultant posts in the psychiatry of late life and would like to see recognition given to 'psychogeriatrics' as a specialized branch of psychiatry. Their definition of psychogeriatrics is that used in this book, namely the management of all forms of mental illness in the elderly, defined as those aged 65 and over. The psychogeriatrician does not necessarily devote his whole time to the psychiatry of the elderly, but may deal with psychiatric conditions in all age groups. However, he does accept a commitment not only to the individual mentally ill old person, but to the provision of a comprehensive service for this group of people, and thus to collaboration with others, such as geriatricians and Social Service Departments, providing cognate services.

RESOURCES

Policy for the mentally infirm elderly is still largely that laid down in the document HM 72 (71) (DHSS 1971*a*) to which reference has already been made. This stipulated that between 2·5 and 3 beds per 1,000 of population aged 65 and over were required for 'elderly patients with severe dementia', while those with functional mental illness or with accompanying physical disease were to be accommodated in the resources already provided for the ordinary psychiatric and geriatric services. These figures have been justly criticized as quite insufficient by the members of the Group for the Psychiatry of Old Age of the Royal College of Psychiatrists. (See also Jolley (1977).) The consequence of this Government policy is that there are not and never will be sufficient mental hospital beds to accommodate all the elderly with mental illness who may require hospital care, and that in consequence many mentally ill old people have to remain at home, or to be housed inappropriately in residential homes, geriatric units, and other unsuitable settings.

HM (72) 71 also recommended that day hospital provision for the mentally infirm elderly should be at a rate of 2 to 3 places per 1,000 of population aged 65 and over. Day hospital care is certainly helpful in many patients in this group, particularly in the relief which it provides for families, but it leaves many problems inadequately solved. In any case this figure has not been attained in most parts of the United Kingdom.

COMMUNITY SERVICES

Some psychogeriatric services have developed programmes in which mentally impaired old people living at home, particularly those living with families, are visited by community nurses based on the local psychiatric hospital or psychogeriatric unit. The continuity of care and the advice which these nurses provide consolidates the family's tolerance. The community nurse reports to the consultant the most appropriate time for relief admission to in-patient or day-patient care.

JOINT PSYCHOGERIATRIC ASSESSMENT UNIT

The function of a joint unit is to provide a meeting place for geriatricians, psychiatrist, and sometimes the Social Service Department, where cases of difficulty and of mutual interest can be evaluated and the best management decision reached. HM (72) 71 recommended a unit of 10 to 20 beds to serve a population of a quarter of a million. The need for such units is limited and they solve few problems since supporting beds have to be found for patients who, after assessment, need additional care. Their greatest value is to provide geriatrician, psychiatrist, and social worker with a working environment in which they learn one another's skills.

Collaboration between geriatric
and psychiatric services

The problems of the elderly with mental illness are best solved when a psychiatrist with a special interest in the elderly works in close collaboration with a geriatrician. In various parts of the country collaboration takes the following forms:

(i) In one or two areas a single office of referral for all elderly patients with physical and mental disability has been established and referrals are apportioned to the geriatrician or to the psychiatrist by mutual discussion from the outset. This arrangement is ideal but requires a common catchment area.

(ii) Several areas have joint psychogeriatric assessment units, in some of which Social Service Departments participate. The right to admit to this unit is vested equally in each of the principals, but the number of beds is limited and there is usually an obligation to transfer the patient elsewhere after a lapse of about four weeks. These units are successful but demand discipline and vigilance for their effective working.

(iii) Regular consultation may take place between the different consultants about individual patients and general management policies.

(iv) Most of the collaboration that exists depends on easy and informal consultation between consultants who are interested in the problem and who respect one another's difficulties.

In many parts of the country communication between the two disciplines is less easy. Difficulties arise where the catchment area of a geriatric unit overlaps with those of more than one psychiatric unit and vice versa. This makes it less convenient for the consultants to confer regularly and to understand each other's difficulties.

Practical difficulties

The most frustrating experience in the care of the elderly with mental illness is when the mechanism for dealing with a crisis cannot be brought into action. A general practitioner may be besieged by relatives under great stress, demanding action because of the no longer tolerable behaviour of a mentally infirm elderly patient. The general practitioner may approach in turn a geriatrician, a psychiatrist, and a social worker, each of whom may have valid reasons for not helping at the time. The general practitioner may solve the immediate problem by arranging the patient's admission to the general medical ward as a real or spurious medical emergency. If the patient's behaviour remains difficult, the general physician is left with the task of going round the three departments in search of help. This should not but does happen, and illustrates the almost unavoidable consequences of lack of resources, poor administrative arrangements, and impaired professional relationships.

Summary
The National Health Service provides specialized facilities for the care of the elderly with mental infirmity. The participation of geriatric, psychiatric, and social services gives the opportunity of selecting the service which best meets the need of the patients, provided that this is not jeopardized by the adoption of defensive stances in the face of resource shortages. The social worker can give most help to her clients when she fully understands the policies of, and the pressures upon, the local geriatric and psychiatric services.

7 DEMOGRAPHIC AND SOCIAL ASPECTS OF OLD AGE

The place of the over-sixties in the population

The number of people in Great Britain aged 60 and over has virtually trebled since the beginning of this century, rising from two and three quarter million in 1901 to over ten million in 1971 (OPCS 1974). It is estimated that 2 to $4\frac{1}{2}$ per cent of these are suffering from mental infirmity (Meacher 1972). A hundred years ago high birthrates and high mortality rates had combined to create a pyramid-shaped population structure with a concentration on younger groups typical of many under-developed countries today. After the 1870s, despite minor fluctuations, the birthrate declined steadily. By 1976, for the first time since the 1930s, the number of deaths slightly exceeded the number of births. During the same period mortality rates declined.

In Great Britain by 1976, of those aged 60 and over one half were aged between 60 and 69, one-fifth between 70 and 74, and one quarter 75 plus: just under 5 per cent were aged 85 and over. By the late 1990s it is anticipated that the percentage aged 60 to 64 will have declined by 8 per cent, while those aged 70 and over will have increased by 23 per cent. In absolute numbers the biggest expansion will be among those aged 75 to 84. These projections would mean that by 1996 people of 75 and over would make up a third instead of a quarter of the total number of old people (OPCS 1976). The frail and dependent, including the mentally infirm, comprise a disproportionate percentage of this group (Kay, Beamish, and Roth 1964).

RATIO OF POPULATION OF OLDER PEOPLE TO
TOTAL POPULATION AND TO WORKING POPULATION

In 1951 people of pensionable age, i.e. men aged 65 and over and
women aged 60 and over, made up 13·5 per cent of the total
population, and children under the age of 15 made up 22·5 per
cent. Comparable figures in 1976 were 17·1 per cent and 22·8 per
cent respectively (see *Table 3*).

Table 3 *Numbers of 15-year-olds and people of pensionable age compared
with the working population in Great Britain 1951/1976*

Age	1951		1976	
	number (thousands)	%	number (thousands)	%
0–14	10,996	22·5	12,438	22·8
15–59 + (women) 15–64 + (men)	31,495	64·0	32,745	60·1
60 and over (women) 65 and over (men)	6,685	13·5	9,359	17·1
total population	49,176	100	54,542	100

Source: OPCS (1976).

The working population declined in relation to the two
dependent sections of the population during this twenty-five year
period. It had a heavier economic burden to carry. The ratio of
pensioners to those of working age is an index of how many each
person in active employment has to support. In 1901, the ratio was
about 10:100; in 1951, it was 21:100, and by the mid 1970s it had
risen to 28:100. Indications are that the rise will continue until
the late 1990s (Grimley Evans 1975).

The economic burden carried by the working population was
increased by the raising of the school leaving age to 16 in 1972,
by more people surviving to pensionable age, and by fewer of them
continuing to work. In 1901 around three-fifths of men aged 65
and over were either working or in search of a job. By 1971, this
proportion had declined to two-fifths (19·2 per cent) (Grimley
Evans 1975). The opposite trend occurred among women. In 1951,
364,000 (7·9 per cent) were working; by 1971 this had gone up

to 744,000 (12·1 per cent) (Wroe 1973). The 1971 census figures show that the percentage of either sex working beyond pensionable age decreases sharply with increasing age.

About half of all elderly people in employment are working part-time; the jobs they do are, on average, of a low socio-economic status. This is particularly true in the case of elderly women, half of whom work in personal service or in unskilled manual occupations (Hunt 1978). High rates of unemployment and the earnings rule* act as disincentives to pensioners who might otherwise continue working. According to a survey conducted in 1976 a substantial minority of both sexes, virtually regardless of the nature of their previous employment, would have liked to have continued to work beyond the age at which they gave up (Hunt 1978). Consequently, some people over retirement age are less well off than they might otherwise be. The disadvantage is not only financial. On retirement some men miss not only their spending money, but the companionship of workmates, satisfaction in the job itself, and loss of a regular routine (Beveridge 1965). One survey showed that a significant number of elderly people on retirement suffered from ill health including depression, apathy, and 'decay of mental faculties' (Grant 1959). A mortality rate of 30 per cent has been recorded for pensioners between the ages of 65 and 70. This rate is significantly higher than for those who retire at later ages (Institute of Actuaries 1958). A more flexible retirement age might help to reduce the incidence of early death among a minority of pensioners (see Kay, Beamish, and Roth 1964).

SEX DISTRIBUTION AND RATIO AT DIFFERENT AGES
In 1901 in Great Britain a baby boy had an expectation of life of 48 years, a baby girl of 51. Comparable rates by 1971 were 68·5 and 75. Women of 80, could on average look forward to an extra seven years of life; men, to only five and a half years (Central Statistical Office 1976). The advantage continued until the mid 1970s (Central Statistical Office 1977).

Women at all ages have lower mortality rates than men. More males than females are born, but the proportions are soon reversed.

---

* The earnings rule. After pensionable age, women under 65 and men under 70 who go on working and earn more than £52.10 per week lose some of their pension for everything they earn above that sum. Women aged 65 and over, and men aged 75 and over, can draw their full pension without restriction on earnings. Such earnings are taxable (November 1979).

In 1975 the mortality rates for men aged 15 to 24 and between the ages of 60 and 70 were approximately double those of women of the same ages. The major cause of death in men in the younger age group was accidents and violence: middle-aged men were more vulnerable to diseases of the circulatory system (see *Figure 2*).

The effect was that in the 45 to 49 age group there were 104 women to every 100 men; in the 60 to 64 group there were 115 women to 100 men; in the 80 to 84 group there were 200 women to every 100 men; and the proportion increased to 300 women to 100 men among those of 85 and over (Age Concern Research Unit 1977). In the group aged 60 and over women outnumber men by almost 50 per cent; after the age of 75 they outnumber them by over 100 per cent. Consequently elderly women make up the bulk of those likely to need support.

MARITAL STATUS BY AGE AND SEX

The marital status of older men compares sharply with that of women. In 1976, 70 per cent of men aged 60 and over had a living partner, compared with 63 per cent of women. Of those aged 75 and over, 59 per cent of men and only 18 per cent of women were still married (see *Table 4*).

Table 4 *Marital status of population aged 60 and over, Great Britain, mid 1976 (thousands)*

age group	men			women		
	married	others	married as % of total	married	others	married as % of total
60–64	1,207	218	86	1,063	551	66
65–69	1,012	226	82	822	716	53
70–74	680	215	76	507	787	39
75 and over	515	356	59	346	1,563	18
total	3,414	1,015	77	2,738	3,617	43
all ages	13,969	12,603	52	13,901	14,069	50

Source: Age Concern Research Unit (1977).

Figure 2 *Selected causes of death by age and sex, Great Britain, 1975*

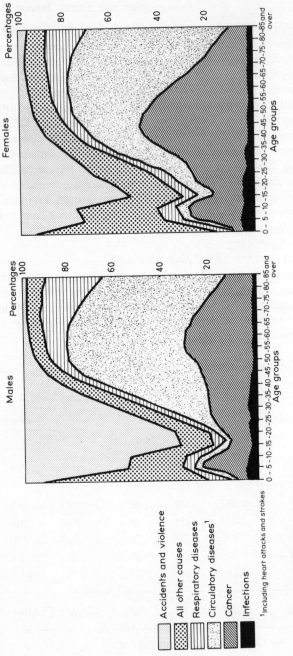

Source: Central Statistical Office (1977a).

Women not only live longer on average than men, but men tend to marry younger women which exposes a large percentage of elderly females to long years of widowhood. On the other hand women become widows at a later age than they did in the early 1900s. Despite an increase in the life expectation of men aged 60, it is not expected that the ratio between the sexes will change during the next twenty years (Age Concern Research Unit 1977). According to current estimates there will be 3·6 million women in Great Britain aged 70 and over by the middle 1990s. Only a quarter of these will be still married.

FAMILY SIZE AND STRUCTURE
Family size has fallen sharply since the middle of the century. In 1871, couples had an average of five children, half had six or more, and fewer than one in ten had no children. By 1921, the average number of children had fallen to two, only 7 per cent had six or more, but twice as many couples as in 1871 (17 per cent) were childless. Higher survival rates have done something to counterbalance this trend (see *Table 5*).

Table 5 *Percentage of adult children surviving to age 45 and average number of children per family 1871/1931.*

year of birth	average number of children	number surviving to age 45	percentage surviving to age 45
1871	4·8	2·7	56
1881	4·1	2·5	60
1891	3·3	2·2	66
1901	2·6	2·0	77
1911	2·2	1·7	77
1921	2·0	1·6	80
1931	2·2	2·0	91

Adapted from Exton-Smith and Grimley Evans (1977: 132).

This general pattern is similar to that in other Western European countries. The decline in family size affects the present generation of old people and will continue to have its impact on future generations. There are and will continue to be fewer close relatives of the same age and fewer adult children available to give help and to share responsibility. This may be partly compensated for by more grandchildren, step-grandchildren and even great-grandchildren (Age Concern Research Unit 1977). Although half the population of pensionable age is widowed, between 40 per cent and 50 per cent are estimated to have one or two children, 80 per cent to have surviving brothers or sisters, and 90 per cent to have at least one grandchild (Shanas *et al.* 1968). The majority of old people have good potential family resources for help but this position deteriorates with increasing age.

On the other hand, there is a vulnerable minority estimated to be between a fifth and a quarter of the total, who either have never married or though married, or once married, are now childless. They find themselves increasingly socially isolated if they lose sisters, brothers, or their partners (Shanas *et al.* 1968). Evidence on mentally infirm elderly women living in the community suggests that more of them than 'normal' elderly women are very old, (average age 77·7, compared with 72·1) widowed, single, and likely to be socially isolated. Further, both men and women suffering from mental infirmity are more likely than normal groups to have few and declining social contacts, to have been unemployed for over five years, to have lower incomes and homes with poorer amenities (Kay, Beamish, and Roth 1964). On the other hand, according to recent research, living in a multi-generation household seems to prevent, or at least to delay, the onset of mental deterioration (Parsons 1965). This suggests that the mentally infirm are more likely to be drawn from the minority group without family support than the majority with it.

HOUSEHOLD COMPOSITION

In 1971, 8·3 million men and women over pensionable age lived in private households. 2·2 million of these lived on their own; 2·7 million with a married partner who was over pensionable age; 700,000 with a partner under pensionable age, and the remaining 2·7 million in other types of households (Wroe 1973). 26 per cent of the total population over pensionable age lives alone, and 84 per cent of these are women. This form of isolation increases steeply for those aged over 75, an age group dominated by women (see *Table 6*).

Table 6   *Elderly population living in private households, Great Britain, 1971 (thousands)*

household type	pensionable age to 75 years				age 75 or over			
	men nos.	%	women nos.	%	men nos.	%	women nos.	%
living alone	210	11·1	1,188	27·8	142	19·1	658	42·7
living with spouse	1,207	64·1	1,862	43·7	402	54·0	349	22·7
living with never married child(ren)	48	2·6	294	6·9	43	5·8	179	11·6
living with spouse & never married child(ren)	285	15·1	468	11·1	91	12·2	139	9·0
other household types	134	7·1	444	10·5	67	8·9	216	14·0
total persons	1,884	100·0	4,256	100·0	745	100·0	1,541	100·0

Quoted in Age Concern Research Unit (1977).

In 1975 in Great Britain, two-thirds of both men and women living in private households who had been but were no longer married, lived alone. Those who had never married were less likely to live on their own (48 per cent) (Central Statistical Office 1977).

The size of the average pensioner household is very small – eight out of ten married couples live alone. On the other hand, households where the head is not yet retired rarely include people over the age of 65 (Department of Employment 1977). This bleak picture of social isolation in old age is relieved by evidence from sociological sources. Visiting relatives give some form of help and companionship to four out of ten elderly people, and seven out of ten receive visits from friends. Bedfast and housebound elderly people are unfortunately less likely than the more mobile either to have living relatives or to receive visits from friends (1 in 7 neither receive nor go on visits compared with 1 in 50 in general) (Hunt 1978). According to one survey two-thirds of old people have relatives including adult children who, though they do not live within the same dwelling, do live in the same household or in the same building, or within a thirty-minute journey of the old person's home (Townsend and Wedderburn 1965). More recently, Abrams (1978) has confirmed evidence of frequent family contacts even for those who are living alone.

According to the 1971 census, about 6 per cent of people aged 65 or over live in institutions. This percentage increases from 3 per cent of those aged 65 to 74, to 8 per cent of those aged 75 to 84, and to 21 per cent of those aged 85 and over. Over two-thirds of the institutions were either hospitals or homes for the elderly.

SUPPORT FROM THE FAMILY

Family help is a reciprocal affair; old people are not just the recipients of services and gifts. The pattern of family support has altered in the last decade from the one recorded by Townsend in the late 1950s (Townsend 1963). The help he described centred on a close-knit slum community with grandmother helping her daughter and grandchildren, and vice versa. The extended family offered mutual support and was easily accessible. Grandparents tended to be within easy reach, sometimes living in the same building as their children, but rarely by choice in the same household. Help tended to be given through the female line and included using influence to get a house or new job as well as help with the domestic chores. The situation has now changed. It has become more like that described by Bell (1968) as typical of middle-class families. In such families, the chain of help is said to run through the male line. Social mobility is central to the middle-class life-style and the family tends to be geographically scattered, making it difficult to give mutual help. Adult children may profit from generous gifts or loans from their parents, from help in clothing and educating their children, and from the use of influence in getting a job or furthering a career.

The 1976 survey (Hunt 1978) shows that four out of ten (41·5 per cent) of old people receive help from their relatives. Women do so more frequently than men, the older more than the younger groups, and those living alone more than those living with others. Over half the people interviewed were visited by a relative at least once a week, or more frequently (54·4 per cent). Worst off were Londoners, whose young relatives have moved away, and those living in retirement areas, who have themselves moved. Over one quarter would have welcomed more frequent visits from relatives. Housebound and bedfast people, who rarely live alone, have a still greater need.

On the other hand, one-fifth (21·9 per cent) of the old people were themselves able to give help to relatives, though their capacity declined steeply with increasing age. Problems arise when parents can no longer manage on their own as the distance that separates them from their families makes regular practical help impossible. The solution may involve two generations sharing a home, which is not always welcome, each family recognizing the integrity of marriage and seeking to keep an independent home. In 1975 in Great Britain 14 per cent of elderly married couples, 15 per cent of widowed men and women, and 17 per cent of divorced or separated men and women lived with their children (Central Statistical Office 1977).

The shift from independence to increasing dependence does not usually occur until old people reach the age of at least 75 (see Townsend and Wedderburn 1965; Sheldon 1948). Between 75 to 84 there is a decline in mobility, health, social contacts, and ability to perform personal and domestic tasks. After 85 this decline normally accelerates. Failing health is a particularly common cause for no longer married elderly people moving into the household of a married child (Shanas *et al.* 1968). Even so, many elderly people living with younger relatives make an appreciable contribution towards household expenses (Hunt 1978).

A minority of the frail elderly fail to get help from at least one of their adult children. This minority appears to be made up of those who, as young parents, tended to treat their children with coldness, cruelty, or indifference. It is more common to find children striving to help their failing parents until they die, sometimes at over-whelming cost to themselves (Isaacs, Livingstone, and Neville 1972). One survey showed that three-tenths of the close relatives living separately provided daily help to a dying person; and nine out of ten living within the same household, gave daily nursing and other care. There appeared to be an informal network of relatives and friends who worked together to give support to the dying (Cartwright, Hockey, and Anderson 1973).

There is a tiny minority of elderly people who exhaust even the most loving and generous care of their adult children. This group includes an excess of women suffering from incontinence and brain failure. Long-term nursing, loss of sleep, and incompre-

71

hension of the old person's regressive behaviour leads to the adult child's refusal to continue to carry the burden.

HOUSING CONDITIONS

According to population estimates in the mid 1970s of the large conurbations, only Greater London had more elderly people than the national average (14·3 per cent compared with 14·1 per cent) (OPCS 1976). Overall the big conurbations do not contain a disproportionate number, and the West Midlands has only 12 per cent. However, each of the Metropolitan Counties does have a higher proportion of older people in its inner-core areas and relatively few in the more desirable outer suburbs. There are an excess of retired people living on the South and South West Coasts (Age Concern Research Unit 1977). Roughly one-third of people aged 65 and over live in property which was built before 1919, one-third in houses built in houses since 1945 (Hunt 1978). One-third have lived at their current address for over thirty years (Wroe 1973). Elderly people live in houses which are older than average and which have fewer basic amenities, such as a fixed bath, an internal WC, or adequate heating facilities. The condition of individual homes both externally and internally is markedly low for those aged 85 and over, for private tenants, for those living in the London area, and for single and divorced people (Hunt 1978). Substandard housing is a measure of deprivation which is linked with poor health, with shortage of open spaces, heavy traffic flow, narrow streets, and decaying buildings (Holman 1970). It also means more hazards which could lead to accidents. This sort of environment can combine with personal circumstances to create misery and to undermine self-confidence.

Over three-fifths of households with elderly heads occupy whole houses. Some old people, more frequently owner-occupiers than council tenants, can be burdened with a family house which is too big. Only a minority live in specially designed council dwellings. Elderly people living alone and those aged 85 and over are more likely than others to be living in old peoples' dwellings, but even in these groups only one in seven do so (compared with one in twelve of all elderly) (Hunt 1978). The Cullingworth Committee has called for a flexible local authority housing policy designed to give the very old, regardless of whether they were previously council tenants, a manageable home, preferably within easy reach of relatives (Ministry of Housing 1969). Rehousing on the top floors of tower blocks could only add to their problems by increasing the danger of social isolation.

INCOME

As *Table 7* illustrates, the average weekly income of people of pensionable age in 1975 ranged from less than £50 to more than £80. All types of elderly households had lower average incomes than those where the head was not retired. The most prosperous elderly households consisted of one man and one woman. Even they had an average gross income that was little more than half that of the non-retired household (£42.70 compared with £84.31). However, when average incomes were translated into average incomes per head, the contrast was greatly reduced. On this basis the poorest elderly household type was made up of a woman and a man aged 65 and over whose income per capita was 80 per cent of the average per capita income of non-retired households (Age Concern Research Unit 1977). On the other hand, the group with the largest per capita income was the unmarried man living alone whose gross income was almost as much as that for the average family where the head was under pensionable age and still working. These figures should be interpreted with caution, because all household expenses have to be met by one income in the case of the man living on his own, but can be shared within a family. They also take no account of fringe benefits and other expenses which supplement the real income of many employed people.

The main source of income of elderly households is provided by national insurance and supplementary pensions. In Great Britain in 1971, 2·2 million (28 per cent) of the 7·4 million pensioners drawing state pensions were also receiving the supplement (Wroe 1973). Two-thirds of them were women. A further 0·5 million pensioners qualified for the supplementary pension but did not apply, despite publicity encouraging them to do so.* Social security benefits made up between 45 per cent and 62 per cent of the average total incomes of elderly households, compared with only 5 per cent of incomes where the head was below retirement age (Department of Employment 1977). According to the 1976 Survey 17·2 per cent of elderly couples were entirely dependent on the state retirement pension with or without supplementary benefit (Hunt 1978).

* In 1975, 600,000 pensioners who were entitled to benefit did not claim it. Estimated benefit unclaimed was £65,000,000.

Table 7 *Weekly household income where head is retired, 1975*

weekly household income	% of total households	average number of persons per household	proportion of household members at work %	proportion of household members who are male %	average age of household
£10 to £14.99	11·5	1·00	–	20	73
£15 to £19.99	25·1	1·06	1	18	73
£20 to £24.99	15·3	1·62	2	42	72
£25 to £29.99	11·0	1·78	3	45	73
£30 to £39.99	12·8	1·80	7	42	72
£40 to £59.99	11·1	2·04	19	38	72
£60 to £79.99	7·0	2·43	31	47	71
£80 or more	6·2	2·59	37	46	72
all groups	100·0	1·61	11	37	73

Source: Department of Employment (1977).

In 1975 the main supplement to state pensions was income from investment and occupational pensions; indeed, for the man of 65 or more living on his own, they provided him with one-third of his total income and accounted for his relative affluence (Central Statistical Office 1976). The total of elderly households included two extremes. 13 per cent, usually those with at least one member in full-time or part-time work, had an income of at least £60, and 37 per cent, mainly women living alone, had incomes below £20. The income per head of the latter group was half that enjoyed by the former. In the 1976 survey, half the elderly couples living on their own had net incomes of less than £1,500, and over two-thirds of elderly persons living alone had incomes of less than £1,000 per year (Hunt 1978). There was a marked decline in income levels with age; women's incomes were lower than men's at all stages. Bedfast and housebound old people were less well off than active old people. This was particularly marked in the case of married couples where one partner was housebound. In regional terms, incomes were above average in Greater London and in the South East and South West, and below average in the North West and West Midlands. Even in the highest income groups an appreciable proportion of old people were concerned about finance. According to recent evidence, elderly people with lower incomes were also less well off in terms of household amenities and equipment. Further, they suffered more ill health and were less able to enjoy the positive aspects of life (Abrams 1978; Hunt 1978).

EXPENDITURE

The average weekly expenditure of pensioner households in 1975 was less than half that of the non-retired households (Department of Employment 1977). However, when allowance was made for difference in household size, the money spent per person was very similar (£18.14 compared with £19.58 per head). There were differences in the way each group spent its money. Pensioners, especially the 37 per cent with low incomes, spent over half on food, fuel, and housing. Retired people gave priority to buying food and, on average, were adequately nourished. More prosperous pensioners like non-retired householders, spent less on the three basic necessities and more on clothing, durable consumer goods, alcohol, and transport (see *Table 8*).

Expenditure, like income, declines with age. Those aged 70 and over, who tend to be the poorest, spend less on drink, tobacco,

Care of the Elderly Mentally Infirm

Table 8 *Average weekly expenditure of retired and non-retired households, 1975*

commodity or service	head retired		head not retired	
	£	% of total expenditure	£	% of total expenditure
housing	5.29	18·1	7.72	12·4
fuel, light, power	2.52	8·6	3.13	5·0
food	7.9	27·3	15.19	24·5
alcohol	1.11	3·8	3.32	5·3
tobacco	0.93	3·2	2.26	3·6
clothing	2.07	7·1	5.57	8·9
durable consumer goods	1.51	5·2	4.79	7·7
other goods	2.10	7·2	4.76	7·6
transport	2.49	8·5	9.07	14·7
services	3.17	10·8	6.06	9·7
miscellaneous	0.05	0·2	0.38	0·6
total	29.23	100·0	62.28	100·0
persons in household	1.61		3.18	
expenditure per head	18.14		19.58	

Source: Department of Employment (1977).

clothes, durable household goods, and transport (Age Concern Research Unit 1977). Consequently if the prices of food and fuel go up faster than those of transport and personal and household goods, the poorest group of retired householders are hardest hit and the quality of their life is further diminished.

Elderly people less often own a telephone, a car, a freezer, or full central heating, than do the middle-aged. These recent products were either unavailable when they were still working, or required considerable initial outlay and subsequent upkeep. Groups who are more likely to need a telephone for emergencies, or for social contacts, such as those living alone, or those aged 85 and over, are less likely to have one. The same is true of car ownership. The situation may improve in twenty years' time. Among households with elderly heads, the decrease in the level of ownership of these domestic items is very striking (Hunt 1978).

One way in which pensioners are at an advantage is that they more frequently own their own homes, having in all but a few instances, paid off their mortgages. (40 per cent to 50 per cent ownership compared with 23 per cent to 30 per cent middle aged) (Age Concern Research Unit 1977).

Social commentary

The majority of old people, especially those less than 75 years of age, are usually physically and mentally alert and have more in common with the middle-aged working population than the minority of dependent and frail elderly people. They should not be labelled in a way that implies lessened competence. Their circumstances should be as similar as possible to those prevailing before they reached pensionable age. They should have the opportunity of continued work (together with a higher tax threshold on income and an adequate retirement pension) which would simultaneously prolong healthy life and reduce the economic burden on the working population. The aim would be to keep this majority fit and able to help itself. A secondary gain would be to free increasing numbers of pensioners to inspire and to man services and self-help groups designed to promote the welfare of those older or more frail than themselves. Nevertheless, even though those aged 65 to 74, who account for two-thirds of the elderly population, have a great deal in common with the age group immediately below their own, they include a small percentage in need of help of some kind. In absolute numbers, this may represent as many as the much larger percentage of vulnerable people in the upper age groups (Hunt 1978).

Many of those under 75 do not consider themselves to be elderly. All but a few are able to go out without assistance and have good general health. They are able to tackle all domestic tasks except those which involve heavy work or climbing. About three out of ten are widowed. After 75, there is a decline in powers and an increase in dependence (see Shanas *et al.* 1968; Townsend and

77

Wedderburn 1965). Some individuals escape this altogether. However, half of those aged 75 to 84 are widowed and their health and mobility tend to decline, their range of social contacts and interests falls off, their housing and amenities are lower, and their attitudes to life are less optimistic. On such evidence, if old age must begin anywhere, 75 seems more justifiable than either 60 or 65.

After this significant birthday, an increasing number of people begin to need more support. If they have adult children, they turn first to them or to other close relatives. The vast majority of help given to old people is given by their families, not by the statutory or voluntary services. There are about six times as many mentally infirm old people in private households as there are in hospitals.* A major aim should be to support relatives in their efforts and to reduce strain upon them. It can be achieved by such methods as encouraging a flexible housing policy designed to enable very old people to live near their children; by supplying aids and services directed to reduce the burden of nursing; by providing payment to relatives for their care; by ensuring a system of night and holiday relief, and by offering counselling services where there is friction, stress, or bereavement (see pp. 142–5 for details).

Although the great majority of pensioners are either independent or supported by their families, about a quarter are socially isolated and vulnerable to illness or incapacity. This group includes a predominance of women, particularly those without husbands or close relatives, who are very old, (at least 75 and sometimes over 80), and who are living alone. It includes the physically sick, the disabled, and the mentally infirm. These are priority groups as far as the social and health services are concerned. They include those most at risk in the community and most likely to end their days in some kind of institutional care.

In so far as there is a problem in old age, it appears to have five main causes. First, an increase in the proportion of pensioners in the population and particularly of those aged 75 and over. Second, a higher incidence of physical and mental disease after the age of 65. Third, a failure to give retired people a high-enough income and comparable living conditions with working people. Fourth, a failure to give priority treatment to those most at risk in their

---

* Parsons (1965) found that 4·4 per cent of old people (65 and over) in his sample study in Swansea were 'demented'. This provides a ratio of 6·3 demented elderly living in private households for every 1 in hospital. See also Kay, Beamish, and Roth (1964).

declining years, and fifth, a failure to provide for the needs of the very old and particularly for those without family support. There is a need for an overall social policy to co-ordinate existing efforts to deal with these problems and to develop ways of satisfying unmet needs. Speedy solutions should be sought as the survival of more people to the age of 75 and over will increase the size of the problem.

Summary

The majority of old people up to the age of 75 live independently and have a great deal in common with the age group immediately below their own. However, a minority of them do need community help. After 75, there is a decline in powers and increase in dependence. The majority still get support from close relatives. The most vulnerable of the very elderly are women without husbands, childless or single people, the socially isolated, the physically frail or incapacitated, and the mentally infirm. These priority groups need special help from the health and local authority social services. The size of this problem is increasing and requires urgent action.

8 SOCIAL SERVICES FOR THE ELDERLY

Statutory requirements and the social services

Even the earliest poor relief included help to the ill, indigent, and elderly either through the distribution of charity or through the provision of almshouses. From the early seventeenth century there was a comprehensive system administered through the parishes. This came under increasing pressure because all but the smallest rural parishes outgrew the parochial machinery (Parker 1965). The 1834 Poor Law Amendment Act set up unions of parishes with elected guardians and central control by Poor Law Commissioners. The aim was to stop outdoor relief and to offer instead maintenance in a workhouse with a standard of living that, the Act stated, 'shall not be made really, or apparently, so eligible as the situation of the independent labourer of the lowest class'. The principle of lesser eligibility and the enforcement of the workhouse test, although widely evaded, remained the theoretical basis of the Poor Law administration. They accounted for the shame attached to admission to the workhouse (Inglis 1971). The Poor Law provided help after destitution occurred and failed either to do preventive work or to realize that destitution could depend on misfortune rather than moral failure.

Until the Local Government Act, 1929, the Poor Law and the local authority services ran in separate channels. This Act abolished the local Boards of Guardians and transferred their functions to the major local authorities. At the same time hospitals were transferred from public assistance administration to local authority health committees, and medical and social services were developed for a variety of groups with special needs including blind persons, the

80

mentally defective, and physically handicapped (see Appendix 1, p.161 for relevant sections of the Local Government Act, 1929). The National Assistance Act of 1948 completed the break up of the Poor Law. The local authorities were made responsible by Part 3 of the Act for the care of old people and the welfare of the handicapped. Financial need was met through the National Assistance Board and local authorities were required to provide residential accommodation. They were also given discretionary powers to give grants to voluntary organizations to provide meals and recreational activities to those in need because of age and infirmity. The emphasis for the next decade still tended to be on improving the lot of people living in former workhouses.

Later legislation concentrated more on community services. In particular, the Health Services and Public Health Act, 1968, enabled local authorities to promote the welfare of elderly people in their own homes and to assist voluntary organizations in the same task. Help available included visiting and advisory services, the provision of information, meals, recreation, transport, practical assistance in the home, and of warden services for private and local authority housing. This Act also required local authorities to provide a home help for sick, disabled, and aged people and it enabled them to provide laundry facilities (see Appendix 1, p.161 for list of main legislation governing work of the Social Service Departments).

The present functions of the Social Service Departments in England and Wales were laid down, with some subsequent minor amendments, in the Local Authority Social Services Act, 1970. This incorporated the recommendations of the Seebohm Report (Report of the Committee on Local Authority and Allied Personal Social Services 1968). The Act required local authorities to set up a new department to meet the social needs of individuals, families, and communities, by the amalgamation of the children's department, the welfare department, that part of the health department dealing with the mentally ill and handicapped, and elements from the education and housing departments. The aim was to provide an integrated social service department with an effective family service. The responsibility for the provision of a Home Help service passed from the local Health Authority to the newly constituted Social Service Department. Ideally the service was to be community based, instead of dealing with the problems of individuals and families on a client-group basis.

Further changes in the law added to the function of the Social Service Departments. In 1972 the Local Government Act, and in 1970 the Chronically Sick and Disabled Persons Act, encouraged local authorities to provide a wider range of services to the disabled, of whom a large percentage are elderly. In the National Health Service Reorganization Act, 1973, health service social work staff were transferred to the local authority.

COMPULSORY REMOVAL FROM HOME

The National Assistance Act, 1948, Section 47, as amended by the National Assistance (Amendment) Act, 1951, gave the then medical officers of health (community physicians) power to remove people to hospital or some similar, suitable place. This action is rarely taken – only around 300 old people a year are compulsorily removed to residential accommodation (Willmott 1967). No one can be removed from home because she is old or frail; it is only if she is not being properly cared for and is living in very bad conditions. In order to take action under this section, the community physician has to get permission from his local authority to apply to the magistrates (in Scotland to the Sheriff) for a removal order. Normally seven days' notice must be given to the person who is subject of such an order or to anyone who is in charge of her. The Court Order lasts for not more than three months at a time, and names the place to which the person may be sent.

If an emergency arises, the community physician or other medical practitioner can, without giving the usual seven days' notice, apply directly to the magistrates courts or to a single justice for an emergency order which lasts for three weeks. Application for revocation of such orders may be made but only after six weeks from the date of the first order (see Appendix 1, pp.166–7).

The doctor has to certify that action is being taken in the interest of the person concerned, or is designed to prevent injury to the health of, or serious nuisance to, someone else. Orders apply to people who have neglected themselves because they suffer from a physical handicap or from grave chronic disease, to those suffering from infectious diseases of specific kinds and to people suffering from severe mental disorder. Such powers are used as a last resort and with great reluctance. The local authority must look after the property of anyone subject to a Removal Order if there is no one else to take on the responsibility. It can recover reasonable expenses for this service.

Organization of the community services

There are 174 Social Service Departments in England and Wales under the Department of Health and Social Security (see Butterworth and Holman 1975).* The way in which these departments are organized depends partly on the size of the district they have to cover. The district is normally divided into areas. Seebohm suggested an optimum population of 50,000 to 100,000 for each area served by a team of at least ten to twelve social workers. Social Service Departments operate through these area teams which are responsible for the social needs of the local population. Depending on the size of the area they serve, such a team may comprise a team leader, a deputy, career grade social workers, one or more senior social worker, some basic grade social workers with support from unqualified social workers, welfare assistants, and other ancillary and voluntary workers.

The team collaborates with voluntary organizations which may be partly or wholly funded by the local authority. Other services are offered by voluntary bodies alone. In rare instances additional help is available to members of the community through local authority social workers attached to group practices or to health centres. They work with the primary health care team and often receive referrals of elderly patients from them.

Hospital-based social workers should be better able, as members of the same Social Service Department, to help to promote collaboration between colleagues in the Social Service Departments and workers in the health service. Their joint efforts can be directed to help elderly people who have become mentally or physically ill and who need short- or long-term medical treatment before returning to their own homes.

Referrals may be made direct to the central office of the Social Service Department, to an area office, or to a social worker employed in a hospital or a GP practice. They vary from simple requests such as for meals on wheels, to urgent appeals for help from neighbours or relatives anxious about the strange behaviour or the physical state of an elderly person. Later chapters describe the challenge involved in giving skilled social work to mentally infirm old people and to their supporting relatives and friends (see Chapters 10 and 11).

* The structure of the Social Services in Scotland is different. It is governed by the Social Work (Scotland) Act, 1968. See also the University of Edinburgh Report (1969) *Social Work in Scotland* from the Scottish Council of Social Service.

Range of community services

In the last twenty years, both central and local governments have been in favour of a rapid expansion in services which keep old people in their own homes as the best and cheapest way of taking care of them (see Ministry of Health 1957). Old people almost always prefer such services, but whether they are cheaper or not depends on the degree of attention needed and the period of time for which they have to be supplied (Opit 1977). Between 1970 and 1975 personal social services taken by local authorities to the homes of the elderly more than kept pace with the growth in numbers of those requiring such services (Central Statistical Office 1976a, 1977).

The following list of facilities, aids, and services is designed to give a picture of the range and scope of work which can be undertaken by Social Service Departments, or voluntary bodies, or the two in collaboration.

HOME HELP SERVICE
This is probably the most important single community service which is run by the Social Service Departments. The number of home helps in England rose from 20,000 to 88,065 between 1959 and 1976 (DHSS 1977). The proportion of elderly people in England and Wales assisted by home helps between 1970 and 1975 rose by a third. By 1975 more than 8 per cent of the population aged 65 and over received this benefit and the percentage was continuing to rise (CSO 1976a, 1977).

In spite of this expansion, the service does not meet the demand for help nor is it distributed evenly over the country (Bosanquet 1975). In some instances the allocation of resources within the same service is poor, one person being in desperate need and another still receiving help she no longer requires (Dowdell 1976). A recent report estimated that the gross cost of providing a home help was 85p an hour (Opit 1977). About 94 per cent of these workers are part-time and do not normally work either in the evenings or the weekends.

Their duties include cleaning, washing, shopping, and helping with personal toilet. They may pay bills, collect pensions, and fetch medical prescriptions. Sometimes an individual will help a group of elderly occupants of flats or bungalows. A minority of specialists, who are paid marginally higher rates, may take on additional responsibilities for 'difficult' elderly clients, including undertaking simple nursing. In cases of extreme neglect, two or three may constitute a 'dirt squad' who restore order to neglected premises. In such instances, before a regular home help is assigned, the mental state of the elderly person ought to be investigated and medical treatment obtained.

A mentally infirm old person, in urgent need of help, is not always willing to accept it. She may be proud of her home, however neglected it appears to others. A great deal of patience and tact may be necessary to reduce her resistance. Sometimes the problem is only solved after the home help has been introduced and rapport established.

Home helps are more than cleaners. They can act as a vital link with social and health workers; yet they must not be trained so far beyond their cleaning role that they become an extra member of the caring profession, and forget to dust the sideboard. A useful supplement to the natural skills of these workers would be a Home Help Handbook containing facts about existing services and easy access to supervisors for speedy advice and support on the job. A charge for home helps, depending on the old person's income, may be made for this service. The return appears to be so small that it might be more economical to supply it free (see Dowdell 1976).

DELIVERY OF MEALS

A meals-on-wheels service provides a basic element in the community support programme. It was pioneered by the WRVS, but is now provided by either the local authority Social Service Department or by voluntary agencies with or without its financial support. Meals can be served either in the old person's home or in luncheon clubs which provide company as well as food. The latter are particularly popular in Scotland. The number of meals served to the elderly in England and Wales, measured in terms of the rate per 1,000 aged 65 and over, has increased by more than 60 per cent between 1970 and 1975. This expansion was primarily due to meals being given to more people rather than more meals to the same number of people (see CSO 1976a; Appendix 9).

The meals service, for which a charge is made, is expensive to provide, may be erratic instead of regular, and the nutritional value of the meals is not always high (CIPFA 1974; Davies *et al.* 1974). The most common number of meals served per week in England in 1976 was two per person (see Appendix 9, *Table 9*). The delivery of meals, particularly when five or more a week are required, taxes the service at a time of rising petrol costs. Some areas have attempted to overcome this problem by paying a neighbour to provide a meal for an elderly person, or to supply one which has been pre-cooked and frozen by the local authority. It requires skill and tact to reduce or discontinue this service when the recipient recovers sufficiently to cater for herself once more.

VISITING SERVICES

It is the duty of local authority social workers to inform elderly people of services available and to encourage them to accept the help they need whether it is provided by the Social Service Department, or by voluntary services working alone or in collaboration with the statutory body. Social workers help to provide a safety net for old people who are in danger of isolation or of neglect by arranging regular visits. Evidence suggests that 'welfare supervision' of the elderly receives low priority in Social Service Departments and is usually delegated to welfare assistants or volunteers. It is a vital way of recognizing need, marshalling help, and avoiding crisis situations, particularly when very old people become suddenly frail or mentally infirm (see Age Concern 1973).

SOCIAL AIDS

The number of households receiving assistance from the Social Service Departments doubled between 1973 (150,000) and 1976 (317,200) (CSO 1977; Appendix 9, *Table 9*). The local authority may under the general heading of 'promoting the welfare of old people', provide aids and other services designed to make life easier for those who are handicapped (see Appendix 9, *Table 10*). These include simple aids such as stocking pullers and long-handled shoehorns, wheeled trolleys, and adapted garden tools, as well as specially designed cutlery and kitchen equipment. Adaptations can be made to the home to provide easy access, by ramps, rails, or by widening doorways for a wheelchair. The home can be made safer and easier to manage by adding handrails on stairs, grips beside baths and lavatories, by altering the kitchen, or by adding a downstairs cloakroom. Adaptations can include insulation and improved heating facilities. Occasionally re-housing is a cheaper alternative to the expense of renovating old property.

The local authority can install a telephone and can pay the rentals for those who live alone and require a telephone as a lifeline. Provision of telephones is limited by their cost. The council is also able to help handicapped and elderly in their own homes by offering handicraft instruction and by supplying televisions or radios.

THE OCCUPATIONAL THERAPIST

An occupational therapist in the Social Service Department may visit handicapped people of all ages, including the physically and mentally infirm. She is primarily concerned if their disabilities are increasing, or if they have had a recent illness or operation which has reduced their capacity to live in their own home. She is able to assess the degree of disability suffered, plan a training programme, and provide appropriate aids. Ideally, the training programme involves the old person attending a short-term, rehabilitative residential course. Failing this the occupational therapist arranges a home-based programme. She then co-operates with other members of the social, health, and voluntary services to safeguard the handicapped person (see Ransome 1978).

CHIROPODY

The overwhelming majority (nine out of ten) of those who, in Great Britain in 1976, were helped by this service, were aged 65 and over (CSO 1976a, 1977). Chiropody is available either on direct application or on the recommendation of a GP, district nurse, or social worker. It can be provided by the area health authority or by voluntary bodies. It is free of charge to priority groups such as old and disabled people. In some areas home visits are possible; more commonly it is available at local clinics. Because demand exceeds the supply, there is often a delay before treatment can be given. A private chiropodist, who charges a fee, may temporarily fill the gap. Greater problems arise when old people live in an area where the service is minimal.

LAUNDRY

In cases of extreme need bed linen and a free laundry service can be provided for elderly people by local authorities or by voluntary bodies. This service is only available in a few areas. It is of particular help to those who are looking after incontinent patients. Occasionally linen, disposable draw sheets, and incontinence pads are supplied. They reduce the acute need for a laundry service.

Charges depend on income. Old people, or their relatives, are entitled to special free waste collections when they have to dispose of large quantities of incontinence pads, used dressings, and other medical and nursing waste.

BLIND WELFARE SERVICES
79,000 people of 65 and over were registered blind in England and Wales in 1976 (CSO 1977). Blind and partially sighted people may be referred to the Blind Welfare Services of the local authority. Blindness need not be complete for entry on the local authority register. Those registered qualify for supplementary benefit and special equipment. Together with partially-sighted people they may also benefit from visits from social workers for the blind who can advise about various aids, clubs, handicraft classes, rehabilitation arrangements, and special holidays. National voluntary societies also supply a free lending service of books and periodicals in braille or moon (National Library for the Blind), aids, and rehabilitation courses (Royal National Institute for the Blind).

SERVICES FOR THE DEAF
7,200 people aged 65 and over were registered as deaf in England and Wales in 1976 (CSO 1977). Social workers visit and help as in the case of the blind. Voluntary organizations may act as agents for this work. Advice is given about hearing aids, finger spelling, and lip reading. Relatives are helped to understand problems arising from deafness in the elderly. The service is available to those caring for the mentally infirm who are also hard of hearing.

NIGHT WATCH SERVICE
Social Service Departments and the Red Cross are able, if funds are available, to provide persons to watch over patients at night. These staff are not trained nurses but do provide relief for families who are caring for sick, elderly relatives. It can be of particular help to those who are losing sleep because of the nocturnal wanderings and noisy behaviour of an elderly mentally infirm relative. Relief is available for a limited number of nights and the provision is means tested. A further voluntary service is provided for the home care of patients with terminal cancer, by the Marie Curie Nursing Foundation. It may be grant-aided, but a charge is normally made.

DAY CENTRES AND CLUBS

Local authorities in Great Britain provide over 300 Day Centres for the elderly, while voluntary organizations run several thousand social clubs (Central Office of Information 1977). The local authority can also offer facilities within residential homes. They can provide some centres specifically for the mentally infirm, or the mentally handicapped. Transport difficulties sometimes limit the availability of this service. Most centres are open daily for several hours, providing a cheap midday meal. They may also offer baths, chiropody, and social activities as well as opportunities to do craft work and other hobbies.

Day Centres have several purposes. They help to prevent loneliness. They provide a place where old people can meet each other and get care and attention while a responsible relative is at work. They may be a useful refuge from an emotionally charged home atmosphere. They provide a stimulus to people living alone who would otherwise, because of their isolation, deteriorate mentally. They may enable the elderly infirm to function at a better level (Central Office of Information 1977).

VOLUNTARY ORGANIZATIONS

Voluntary organizations, as well as providing visits for the elderly, play a vital role in their care. They have pioneered housing schemes, provided residential homes, as well as doing work in the local community such as meals-on-wheels, luncheon clubs, day and recreation centres. Voluntary workers may also help in hospital care by the provision of such facilities as library services, canteens, and outings. Sometimes the organizer is paid (see Appendices 5 and 6, pp.187–9).

CHARITIES

Charities are available to help the elderly in a variety of ways. They may pay for dog licences, veterinary fees, budgerigars, radio and television sets. Financial help is often available for those in special need. Some of these funds are local; among the best-known of the national funds are the National Society for Cancer Relief and the Distressed Gentlefolks Aid Association. Information about charities is available either through the local authority legal services' department or by consulting a copy of the Annual Charities Digest published by the Family Welfare Association.

FURTHER SERVICES

For details of financial and other concessions available to elderly people see Appendix 3; for notes on legal services, see Appendix 2.

SOME EXPERIMENTS IN COMMUNITY SERVICE

This list is not meant to be exhaustive. Where possible a name or organization has been attached to each experiment. This does not necessarily mean that it is the only organization which is carrying on the experiment. Experiments flourish and die. The aim here is to give ideas which may be used or adapted in other areas of the country. The services referred to are sometimes collaborative efforts. They include services designed for a different group which might effectively be adapted to meet the needs of the mentally infirm elderly.

Register of old people (Birmingham)

This register was compiled from the (then) City Health Executive Council records. It was originally confined to those aged 75 and over who could tick services required on the form supplied. If registers were compiled throughout the country, this would provide the means of discovering the main groups at risk (of which the mentally infirm are a significant example) among the elderly. The principal deterrents at a time of shortages are cost and availability of resources.

Easy Alert (New York)

This system is run by the City's Department for the Ageing which gives wide publicity to its telephone number. Anyone over 65 may register. A red dot identifies a mail box belonging to an old person. If letters accumulate the local postman telephones Easy Alert which makes enquiries and, if necessary, gives help. In this country the milkman might act as the key person and the Social Service Department as the resource agency.

The Fish Scheme (Oxford)

A voluntary initiative supported by local churches to encourage neighbourliness on a street basis. Vulnerable elderly people are issued with a card with a fish device to display in their front windows in emergencies. Volunteers keep a daily watch ready to take action. A similar scheme based on street wardens was pioneered in Kirkcaldy.

Family Community Care (Norfolk County Council)
and boarding out (Age Concern)
In Family Community Care voluntary workers are recruited by local Social Service Departments and given training and continuous support during their work. For a small wage and maintenance allowance, volunteers offer care in their own homes to elderly people who need a holiday or time to recoup strength after a physical or mental illness. Age Concern and local voluntary service councils have pioneered similar schemes in which volunteers have been asked to 'foster' an old person, adopting him or her as a member of the family. Placement and follow-up is essential. The old person may in some instances be a paying guest. In others the local authority may give financial support.

Good Neighbour Scheme (Liverpool; Ramsgate –
Kent County Council)
The aim of these schemes is to provide modest payment for relatives, neighbours, and friends to give services to elderly neighbours. The tasks are small, ranging from cooking light meals to emptying a commode, taking the dog for a walk, or providing companionship. The payment can make it possible for relatives and neighbours to help care for old people. Recruits include young housewives and recently retired people. Some schemes are run by voluntary bodies such as Age Concern, others are financed by local authorities as in the case of Ramsgate.

Good Companions (WRVS)
This is a practical service offered by volunteers to handicapped and aged people who are finding it increasingly difficult to run their own homes. Volunteers deal with emergency tasks. They sweep snow, keep an eye on safety factors, escort patients to hospital, the optician, or for hearing-aid fittings. They change library books, collect prescriptions, shampoo hair, and do other household chores. They act as a link person with social workers.

Universal Daughter Scheme (Hastings)
Unpaid volunteers, who are sympathetic practical women with common sense, are recruited by a local hospital in Hastings to befriend lonely elderly people during their hospital stay. They visit, help with shopping, bed-making, and with family transport. They

91

act as a link with professional social workers or other volunteers. A similar scheme could be used to help confused elderly people.

Crossroads Care Attendants Scheme (Rugby)

This scheme was sponsored by ATV with the dual aims of reducing stress in the family of a disabled person and of avoiding hospital admission due to misadventure within the family circle. Volunteers seek to relieve the main carer from unremitting toil. Similar projects could be adapted to meet the needs of confused elderly people and their relatives. The Rugby scheme depends on voluntary funds but it and similar ventures could be subsidized by the local authority. A similar project, known as 'The Flying Angels' operated in Cornwall for many years.

Night duty service (Harrow/Barnet)

Hospital social workers at psychiatric hospitals offer, out of office hours, psychiatric crisis intervention. They are called on a rota basis in conjunction with a consultant. The aim of the team is to alleviate both the psychiatric disturbance and the social problems arising, including reactions of the patient's family. Hospitals may be used as a temporary refuge. This collaborative effort between the health authority and the Social Service Departments could be adapted to help the mentally infirm and their families and to reduce the need for compulsory removal orders.

Relative conferences (Severalls Psycho-Geriatric Unit Liverpool Hospital)

Some hospitals have relatives' conferences in which families meet with consultants to discuss problems and progress. Preparation is made for discharge and support given to relatives when they resume care of the patient. Intermittent hospital admission may be arranged (see Whitehead 1970). Stroke Clubs (Glasgow) have similar aims.

Attachment of social worker to Primary Health Care Team (Birmingham)

A social worker is attached to a local health centre and has direct access to GPs and ancillary health workers. She receives referrals directly from doctors. These tend to include a high proportion of troublesome or disturbed patients as well as those causing concern to relatives and neighbours. This has proved a good way of detecting elderly people at risk in the community.

Reality Orientation Programmes
(Brighton Clinic, Newcastle)

A variety of techniques have been used to stimulate and develop senses and social contacts of elderly mentally infirm people. Very promising results in terms of slowing down the process of mental deterioration and in re-learning lost social skills has been achieved. The effects on residents are positive and staff are encouraged by being able to offer active help to those in their care. The programmes are as applicable to residential homes as to hospital wards (See Mind 1979: 113.)

Hospices (St Christopher's and others)

These include an old person's wing. The aims are to help patients to die in dignity and in acceptance of their state. Help is offered to the families during terminal illness and in subsequent bereavement. 'Care Unlimited', a voluntary group (Tonbridge, Kent) offers a similar service to the dying person and her relatives at home.

Cruse

This is a voluntary organization helping widows with practical, emotional, and social problems. It has developed skills in counselling people at a time of bereavement. Old people may be desperately hit by the loss of a life-time's partner and may deteriorate physically and mentally if no suitable help is available (see Torrie 1975).

Electronic alarm system
(Stockport – Greater Manchester)

1,200 elderly people who are at risk through isolation or disability have been equipped with a small VHF transmitter through which they can summon help. Disabled people can carry a hand-held alarm. A team of mobile wardens are available day or night to respond to calls for help.

Miscellaneous voluntary services

Adopt a Grannie – a scheme in which young volunteers visit regularly, do small jobs, and carry messages.

93

Voluntary Grannie's Helps – a scheme to supplement the home help service.

Running Repairs Help – a group of retired tradesmen or do-it-yourself enthusiasts may, through Task Force or other local enterprises, undertake repairs to old people's homes at modest cost.

Car Help Service – a transport service to help old people to visit a surgery, go to the chiropodist, the out-patients department, the Day Centre, on a specific outing, or on an urgent journey.

A Bakewell Club for the housebound. Members take it in turn to bake, using ingredients supplied by other club members, to whom the final product is distributed.

Food and Friendship Service – the object is to replace or supplement meals-on-wheels. Groups of neighbours eat together in one another's homes to reduce the cost. They also arrange for food to be purchased and cooked by their more fit neighbours for the housebound and handicapped.

Pet Care – a scheme to help old people during illness or hospitalization by caring for their pets.

Residential accommodation

STATUTORY REQUIREMENTS

Residential care has its roots in the Poor Law. The 1834 Poor Law Act, in an effort to discourage pauperism, offered maintenance in a well-regulated workhouse (Parker 1965). The 1948 National Assistance Act brought the Poor Law to an end (see Appendix 1, pp.161–4). In its place responsibility for meeting financial needs was given to the National Assistance Board. The local authority was required to provide residential accommodation for all those 'who by reasons of age, infirmity, or any other circumstances' needed care and attention. The aim was to ensure that accommodation should be a substitute for a normal home, with sufficient clothing, extra comforts, as well as opportunities for recreation and worship. The range of elderly people catered for by the local authority includes active old people, residents who are temporarily indisposed, those who are within a few weeks or months of death and whose removal to hospital would be considered inhumane, and the mentally infirm who may also be partly bed-ridden. Staff are expected to provide care and a degree of nursing support such as would be given by relatives with the help of a community nurse.

Accommodation for the mentally handicapped
and mentally ill

The 1968 Health Services and Public Health Act gave local authorities increasing powers to provide residential accommodation for mentally handicapped people. This includes small homes (twenty to twenty-five beds), flatlets, group homes, and schemes for fostering (see DHSS 1971). The 1959 Mental Health Act gave similar responsibilities to the Social Service Department to offer residential accommodation and 'half-way' hostels to those suffering from or recovering from mental illness (see DHSS 1975).

RESIDENTIAL PROVISION

In 1976, 160,219 people of 65 and over were living in residential accommodation of whom 21,859 (13·6 per cent) were in special homes for the mentally disordered (see Appendix 9, *Table 11*). Seven out of ten (72·3 per cent) of residents in local authority homes were women. Between 1970 and 1975 domiciliary services more than kept pace with the growth in the size of the elderly population, whereas the provision of residential accommodation remained virtually the same. If the age and sex structure of the population is taken into account, the rate in terms of residents per thousand population aged 65 and over was marginally less (CSO 1976a). Consequently, although in 1951 an 85-year-old widow had a reasonable chance of a place in an old people's home, by the 1970s her chances of getting one were remote. She needed to be totally unable to care for herself, and even then she might have to wait for many months before securing admission (Seagrave 1975).

Between 1970 and 1975 the average size of homes fell. In the latter year 7 per cent of residents were living in homes with seventy places or more compared with 12 per cent in 1970 (see Appendix 9, *Table 12*). The most common size of local authority homes was thirty-one to fifty residents. The trend appears to be towards standardization in the middle range with a decline in the number of both large institutions and small homes. This is due to the closure of large poor law institutions as well as of small adapted premises. Some of the newer homes are subdivided into 'family group' units in which bedroom, sitting, and sometimes dining accommodation for a group of about eight to twelve people are clustered together.

SHELTERED HOUSING

The current trend seems to be that group dwellings are particularly popular and may prove suitable for some mentally infirm people. They include group flatlets, warden-supported flats and bunga-lows, and short-term hostel accommodation for those who can manage on their own most of the time. It is less common for tenants from such schemes to move into residential accommodation than it is for frail older people in their own homes (Boldy, Abel, and Carter 1973).

Sheltered housing is a post-war phenomenon, backed by Government advice on planning and design and often linked with a warden service. The warden's job is to make sure that the property is in order, to give advice and information to tenants, to provide emergency services, and to look after the well-being of her tenants. She may also promote efforts to give mutual help and to share leisure time activities among tenants as a whole. The job has much in common with that of residential workers (Brearley 1977).

Sheltered housing and domiciliary services have combined to make it possible for old people, even those with disabilities, to remain in their own homes. The result has been that residential homes are having to care for an increasing number of physically disabled or mentally infirm people and for those whose health has deteriorated with age (see Age Concern 1973, 1974, 1977).

THE RESIDENTS

According to a variety of studies conducted in the 1970s the majority of residents tend to be single, or widowed women of at least 75 years of age (see Brearley 1977). Two-thirds entered the home from the community, where between a third and a half had been living alone (Harris 1968). About 20 per cent came from hospitals, 5 per cent from hotels, lodging or boarding houses, and about 9 per cent from other residential accommodation. About 60 per cent of residents were mentally alert (a situation which is deteriorating) slightly more were fully mobile, 30 per cent were aged 85 or over, and 80 per cent were always continent. More elderly people living in voluntary homes were capable of looking after themselves in a protected environment than were those living in local authority accommodation (85 per cent compared with 67 per cent) (Carstairs and Morrison 1971).

The most common reason for admission was incapacity for self-care as a result of illness. The second largest group was composed of those who had been advised by their doctors to apply because of the danger of their falling or of their being unattended at night. Less than one in ten went into care because of financial difficulties, a wish for companionship, or because of inability to manage physically outside. A high proportion became residents because they had nowhere to live as a result of selling homes or of giving up tenancies on admission to hospital. According to Harris the majority of residents said that they wanted to go into a home; direct applications stemmed most frequently from old people who either did not want to be a burden upon their family, or were unhappy in their present situation because of family quarrels (Harris 1968). A further study suggested that about half of those admitted went into care because they were unable to look after themselves. The remainder applied because they were lonely, had accommodation problems, difficulties in relationships, or, in almost a third of the cases, because they were undermined by a combination of these factors (Wager 1972).

AIMS OF RESIDENTIAL CARE
Residential care offers both group living in various forms and physical support. Where the majority of residents are mobile and mentally alert, the need for physical support is much less. In such instances residents are more in need of being helped to keep as active, and interested in life, as when they were running their own home. Goldsmith (1975) puts it this way: 'Old people don't want everything to be organised for them – there is still a great deal of pride and satisfaction about being able to organise one's own life. This entails having as much freedom of choice open to the elderly as possible. It is often the element of choice which is lacking in an old people's home.' (See also Gibberd 1977.) Total care can lead to total, or near total, apathy where residents quickly assume the characteristics of an institutionalized personality.

Recently efforts have been made to release care staff from burdensome domestic chores so as to free them to pay more attention to the emotional and social needs of residents (see Whitton 1976). Activity programmes have been introduced into certain homes. They are designed to encourage individuals on the basis of an initial assessment on admission, to perform little chores, and to care for themselves as much as they are able. Residents are encouraged to use their faculties to full capacity with the possibility of returning to their own home if circumstances improve. The programme can be modified to accommodate periods of illness or crisis. The aim is to prevent institutionalization and to encourage satisfaction in community life (Whitton 1977). Northampton Social Service Department has converted several traditional homes to ones containing groups of eight people who share, according to individual capacity, the work involved in looking after themselves and their home. The cost of implementing the scheme is minimal and the result on the health and attitude of the residents, remarkable. In particular, confused residents have become active and useful members of the community (see Marston and Gupta 1977).

SEPARATE OR INTEGRATED HOMES
A significant and growing minority of residents in old people's homes are mentally infirm, although the majority are alert and in reasonable health. 12 per cent are classified as 'mentally disordered' (see Appendix 9, *Table 11*). The percentage may well go up to around a third if lesser stages of mental infirmity are included. A local assessment, made in Cheshire in 1975, identified one resident in three as either confused or very confused (Blair, Constable, and Davies 1975). This has led to a controversy about whether separate or integrated homes are best for all the residents. Meacher, who is concerned primarily with mentally infirm old people, has argued in favour of integrated or mixed homes (Meacher 1972). He contends that rational residents often show great patience with confused old people and encourage their reasonable behaviour. Pressures are brought on staff and residents alike to treat mentally disturbed people as adults with rights and wishes which should be respected. Confused old people are less likely in these situations to be treated in a belittling way or exposed to 'infantilizing processes'. Meacher has shown that although mentally infirm old people may appear 'to live in a world of their own', they are not oblivious to slights and snubs and may show acute awareness of how they are being treated. But such integrated homes place a heavy reliance on skilled staff who can create an atmosphere of mutual support. Without it, the behaviour of some confused residents can place intolerable strains on others who have to live in close proximity. Conversely, confused people can be stigmatized and rejected by more rational residents.

Those in favour of segregation of specialist homes argue that, if properly staffed, they may offer more privacy than integrated homes, the opportunity to create a safe, planned environment in which wandering can be contained, and a place where restraint could be reduced to the minimum necessary for safety (Bergman 1973). This would not solve all problems. Confusion is not the only source of either dependency or antisocial behaviour.

A compromise is to have a mixed home with some separate facilities so that rational residents may withdraw and may have a locker or drawer where they can put their valuable possessions. All residents, including the mentally infirm, need somewhere where they can be private and where they can escape the pressure of other personalities.

One of the problems is to use residential accommodation with flexibility. Andrews (1972) has suggested that mentally infirm old people should be divided into four groups. First, there are the frail and very old who need residential accommodation or sheltered housing. The second category includes those with social difficulties like forgetfulness, interfering with others, and wandering tendencies. They should be in local authority hostels for the mentally infirm. The third group are those with acute or chronic physical illnesses who need hospital care in a geriatric ward or unit. Finally, there are those with functional psychoses or neuroses who should be admitted to a psychiatric hospital. Andrews points out that an appreciable number of old people end up in the last two categories of care when they could equally well be treated in one of the two earlier ones. The effect is to reduce the efficiency of the geriatric services in helping a wide range of old people with some form of mental disturbance.

Although increased efficiency is important, mentally infirm people cannot be moved about like pawns. This could lead to deterioration instead of to better care. A possible solution would be to develop a co-ordinated support system, where the expert help of a psychiatrist, geriatrician, or social worker would always be available. The old person would then receive specialist help without being disturbed by a move into a strange environment. Making the right choice about treatment and co-ordinating plans would be a skilled job.

Summary
Early statutory efforts to help the ill, indigent, and elderly concentrated on giving residential accommodation; later legislation has concentrated more on community services. Action to remove an elderly person from her home is taken only exceptionally. She

needs to be not only ill but living in bad conditions and being neglected.

Various facilities, aids, and services, of which the home help and meals-on-wheels are two notable examples, have been developed to try to keep elderly people independent in their own homes. When domiciliary services are not enough local authority residential accommodation can be offered to a range of elderly people including the mentally infirm. There are a variety of types of homes including integrated, separate, and small group homes. Such homes are increasingly occupied by the very old and the most physically or mentally handicapped. Like the domiciliary services they are in short supply.

9 COMMUNICATING WITH ELDERLY PEOPLE

Seek first-hand information

Perhaps the first rule in communicating with old people is that they must be spoken to directly and, unless they are acutely ill and unable to speak for themselves, all information must be acquired first-hand. There is nothing more belittling than being treated like a piece of furniture while relatives are asked, 'How is she today?' or 'Did she have a good night?' 'I had to ask my sister to go out of the room in the end', said one indignant but extremely shrewd 90-year-old. 'The nurse kept asking her what was wrong with me. I can speak for myself – I always have, you know, and I'm not going to stop now!'

Be aware of differences in past experiences

The second major necessity is to be aware of the gap between the past experience and background of the elderly client and the younger social worker. Old people in their seventies and eighties have lived through two world wars and a depression. They can remember the time when state pensions were five shillings, when the Poor Law provided out-relief and medical benefits only after a means test, when residential homes were public assistance institutions, when vagrants made brief stays in the casual wards, when poverty meant the threat of the workhouse, and when unemployment benefit was ten shillings for an able-bodied man.

The following cases quoted in the 1949 Nuffield Report on Old People illustrate the attitude of that day:

(i) Miss A, aged 71, lives with her sister aged 68. Total resources are old age pensions of 10s. a week each and interest on War

Loan amounting to £10 per annum. Refuses to apply for a supplementary pension, although in great poverty and poor health.'

(ii) 'Mr and Mrs B, both aged 74, have a bedridden daughter crippled with arthritis. They struggle to continue work in their shop despite bad health and earn less than if they drew old age and supplementary pensions. They say they would "die rather than undergo the humiliation" of asking for a supplementary pension.'

Another old man described the supplementary pension as 'a charity, and charity stinks' (Rowntree 1947). Though this view was expressed thirty years ago, it is still shared by many elderly people who have seen the liberal march from Poor Laws, to Public Assistance, and on to the Supplementary Benefits Commission – the taste and memory of the old methods of state help linger on. It is essential that social workers understand the source of the resistance they may find to their well-intentioned efforts to get financial or practical help to needy clients. (See Abrams 1978 : 6–7.)

Be aware of age gap
A third obstacle to effective communication is the difference in outlook and attitudes arising from the age gap between old people and their social workers. Because of this, it is important for social workers to be sensitive to subjects which should be treated with reticence. Elderly people grew up in a much less permissive age and were taught 'proper modesty' about sexual behaviour; about avoiding swear words in mixed company; about talking of their financial position or their money problems; and about discussing intimate details of their married life. Because of this, they may sometimes interpret questions in this area in unexpected ways. They may also be shocked or distressed by what they consider to be undue outspokenness. Before the advent of the word, 'loo', to refer to the 'lavatory' or the 'WC' was quite unacceptable to many old people; the 'proper' word was 'toilet' – any other word was as embarrassing to them as unclothed piano legs were reputed to be to the Victorians. Even ten years ago, there were appropriate clothes for informal and formal occasions. Old people are more likely than most to regard with disquiet unusual or exaggerated styles of dress. In their day clothes for work were markedly more sober than leisure clothes. Trendily dressed social workers can cause un-

intentional affront. Misunderstandings can arise where old people's sensibilities are disregarded and these can affect the trust which the client has placed in her social worker. Hence, sensitivity to 'delicate areas' is an important part of facilitating communication.

Take time

A fourth barrier is the difference in pace between social workers and elderly people. Driven by an exacting caseload or by a preference for other age groups, young social workers may present a sense of urgency which is disturbing to an old person who, as one 70-year-old described it, has 'all day to do nothing in'. Indeed, one of the more important processes of ageing involves reaching a new balance in which relationships with others decline and the old person accepts tranquilly a greater detachment from the whirl of social life. A contented detachment of this kind may sometimes be mistaken for loneliness or apathy (Bigot 1970).

However, old people are often a victim of the disease of busyness in others. This includes social workers who appear to have no time to sit and listen, and perhaps unintentionally convey the impression that their foot is itching to step on the accelerator of the car awaiting them at the kerb outside. Relatives and neighbours are often busy with their own lives, and others to whom old people might turn, such as the vicar or the doctor, may have built up such a reputation of industry and overwork for themselves that old people do not like to trouble them (see Wilkes, undated paper). There is a danger that even members of the caring profession may find old age too slow and not take the time to listen, to pause, to seek to understand. Above all, those most at risk of being the victims of busy people with no time are the incurables who may be in danger of scarcely being allowed the time to die in peace. Old age is slow and so is satisfactory communication.

Develop a positive response

A fifth barrier to effective communication may be lack of awareness of the kind of old people most likely to need the help of Social Service Departments. This minority show differences in attitude and behaviour from the lucky survivors with children, relatives, and friends to give company and support. In general terms, the kind of old people who come into contact with Social Service Departments include a disproportionate number of childless, single, divorced, separated, or widowed people and a dispro-

103

portionate number of the over-eighties who are becoming fragile in mind or body and whose support is becoming burdensome to their relatives (see Townsend 1963; Townsend and Wedderburn 1965; Tunstall 1966). Such factors as these are likely to have produced psychological effects in their victims such as depression, a feeling of vulnerability, and low esteem. This group may also contain an excessive number of elderly people who are suffering from loneliness, under-stimulation, or inactivity. They may be grieving for lost powers, for lost status, or most of all, for lost relatives. They may be unduly downcast because of failing powers, irritated and stubborn in their efforts to hold on to a way of life they can no longer sustain, concerned and guilt-ridden at being a burden to others, demanding, and oblivious of how much they are exhausting those who are trying to give them help (Bumagin 1972).

Their tales may be unclear and repetitious and their glance may be darting and suspicious as they seek to judge whether they are being listened to with attention and interest, or indeed, whether they are being listened to at all. Nor do all elderly people relish a dependent role, especially at that stage in their lives when their capacity to give in a reciprocal relationship is less than it was before. They feel at a disadvantage and sometimes behave un-graciously, even truculently. Social workers need to be sensitive to the individual message which is being conveyed. They must try to avoid being alienated, and offer a positive response to even the most apparently hostile old person.

Identify yourself
A sixth hindrance is failure to observe the courtesies when visiting. Older people do not easily accept the more casual manners currently in vogue. Perhaps they are not exceptional in liking a stranger who calls on them to say clearly what their name is, what service they represent, and what is the purpose of their visit. Better still they will appreciate an earlier letter of appointment and an identification card which they can examine on the doorstep before inviting the visitor into their home. Such courtesies give time for older people to adjust and give reassurance if they are nervous of strangers at their door.

Use words with care
A seventh barrier to communication is the misuse of words. Official communications sent through the post to old people usually share

the same fate as gas and electricity bills. They are filed behind the clock or pushed into a drawer in the hope that, if they are forgotten, they will cease to exist or that someone will call to explain them. An unexplained form may arouse the deepest suspicions or defeat the sharpest intelligence, particularly if it opens up to reveal more questions inside. The daunting prose style of many official letters is not reassuring to the old, and letters may, indeed do, give offence if written in an admonitory tone containing unasked-for advice (see Wilkes, undated paper). A personal interview can do much to diminish fears and to calm ruffled feelings. But what if the interviewer talks in an equally obscure fashion? One of the afflictions of the relatively new and aspiring profession of social work is the desire to acquire a technical language with which to impress others.

The context in which words are spoken makes a difference to their meaning. 'Do you feel better?' means quite different things to someone recovering from a cold, to an old gentleman struggling to control his temper, or to an old lady who has recently lost her husband. It seems vital that social workers should think hard about the words they use and make sure they have the same meaning for the old person as they do for themselves. Among the words likely to be misunderstood are 'quarrel' (which to the old person may mean a violent affair) and 'talk' (which may mean a long discussion). Use the word 'unfair' (not 'unjust'); 'smart' or 'intelligent' (rather than 'bright'); 'he was hurt in an accident' (rather than 'injured'); 'I see what you mean' (rather than 'perceive'); 'I want to tell you about that' (rather than 'share information with you'); 'I'll try to explain' (not 'interpret this for you'). If the social worker says 'difficulties in this area' to the old person it may mean 'in this geographical place'. 'Part 3 accommodation', 'discharge', 'admission', or a 'friendly visitor' may be unequivocal phrases to the social worker, but they are likely to be strange, even threatening words to the old person concerned.

Even more significantly sometimes, it is vital to check on local sayings. One senior social worker was puzzled because an old lady said, 'I feel like I'll give my neck'. A colleague later told him that this meant that she was considering committing suicide. The social worker recognized the seriousness of the statement, not from the words used but from its context and the tone of the old lady's voice. Not all misunderstandings are as dangerous as this one could have been. Social workers should read Sir Ernest Gowers' 'The

Complete Plain Words' and be on their guard about the meaning and use of words.

Supplement words with gestures and looks

Social workers' obsession with long words may be a legacy of the emphasis on talking out problems and developing insight which stems from psychoanalytic treatment. Fortunately, verbal messages can be supplemented by facial and body movements which are sometimes a good deal more expressive and more universally understood than words. Leaning forward, smiling, and eye-to-eye contact express warmth and interest, as do nodding and murmuring an encouraging response. Old people often find themselves unnoticed and unheeded. Their social skills may have deteriorated because of lack of practice. Receiving the undivided attention of a visitor may help to build up confidence. Hospitals and homes ought to provide a private room where old people may receive the full attention of their visitors and where a cup of tea may be offered. This not only helps to set people at ease but also gives the old person a chance of contributing to an otherwise unbalanced relationship.

Touch may also be more effective in conveying messages than words. A social worker had been visiting an elderly couple living in their own home. After an interval of a month she called again and was told by the old lady of the death of the husband. She expressed sympathy by taking the old lady's hand and squeezing it. There are many occasions when old people are ill and words are burdensome to them but a gentle touch or a pressure on the hand, may give them comfort. One old lady, who seemed to have lost the will to speak, clearly responded to relatives who came and sat with her, smoothing back her hair and quietly holding her hand. She occasionally reacted with a little squeeze or a pat of her own.

Brearley cites the moving case of Mrs K, an elderly lady of uncertain age, who when visited by her social worker was seen in her front room wearing only her underclothes.

' "She let me in ... We talked about her son and she repeated her usual paranoid ideas about his wife and then became excited ... I had lost the thread of her conversation ... She could see I couldn't understand and became very angry; she burst into tears of frustration. I couldn't think of anything else to do so I put my arms round her shoulders. She held my hand for a little while

and then stood up and dried her eyes and smiled weakly." '
(Brearley 1975: 50)

Auden has warned us:

> 'Some thirty inches from my nose
> The frontier of my Person goes ...'

Social workers ought not without thought to invade another's privacy. They have tended to overvalue words and are only slowly coming to recognize that for certain groups of clients, words are not the most effective means of conveying messages. For example, with elderly people, playing draughts, helping to wind the wool, replacing a light bulb, trimming the budgie's claws, and a host of similar shared jobs may provide the distraction which reduces shyness, makes possible a freer exchange of messages, and helps to develop trust.

Avoid condescension

One of the sad things about growing old is that there are fewer and fewer contemporaries who are sufficiently intimate to call you by your Christian name. This knowledge must never be used as an excuse for using an old person's given name in totally inappropriate settings. Even professional people, intending to be friendly, may be guilty of condescension in the way they address elderly people. Christian names should only be used on a reciprocal basis. There is, no doubt, unintentional superiority conveyed by the speaker when old people are described as 'dears', 'ducks', 'gran', 'old folk', or 'senior citizens', or when 'Darby and Joan' clubs arrange 'OAP outings' for a special group of 'poor old things'. Some people claim to 'love old people', rather in the manner of Mr Tracy Tupman who, it may be recalled, was so fond of the ladies that the very thought brought tears to his eyes. The old, like the ladies, do not greatly care for this feudal way of being loved. We all want to be able to give as well as to take. We all want to be treated as an individual and not lost in a group, especially one which is patronized more than any other in the community.

Make sure your messages are received

Communication is a complex process. It depends on the giver and the receiver of messages each understanding the other with the minimum of distortion, and transmitting and answering messages in an acceptable and understandable form. This delicate transaction cannot take place unless the parties involved have all heard, seen, and 'read' each other aright. This means at the simplest level that old people whose hearing is impaired (and about a third have some difficulty in this area, 6 per cent to a severe extent) may not receive a message correctly because of this defect. Similarly, a fifth of old people suffer from some degree of visual impairment (8 per cent severe) (see Townsend and Wedderburn 1965). They may consequently have difficulty in reading messages and in compensating for deafness by lip-reading, or by keen observation of the body language of their visitor (see McCall's pamphlet, 'Communication Hazards in the Elderly', available from Age Concern). These two sensory disabilities may be further complicated by a decline in alertness and concentration which accompanies the ageing process. It is therefore helpful if social workers can see their clients in a quiet place where extraneous noise is cut to a minimum. If the old people are not in their own homes they should ask to speak to them in a room away from television or radio.

Helping old people to cope with a hearing aid which they are failing to use properly, or helping them to acquire a new hearing aid or spectacles may be an effective way of reducing misunderstandings. The installation of a telephone, where funds allow, will enable elderly housebound people to keep in touch with relatives and friends. Research in Hull has shown how successful this particular aid may be (Gregory and Young 1972).

Receiving messages depends also on the clarity of what is said. Social workers should speak to elderly people clearly and simply and should enunciate precisely so that lip-reading may supplement failing hearing. Dropping the head, mumbling, and making throw-away asides should be avoided. Severe disabilities can lead professional people to mistaken diagnoses. One GP described an elderly patient as 'senile' apparently because she was stone deaf and consequently failed to understand what he was saying to her.

Effective practical help may be a significant first step in the process of improving communication (Goldberg 1970). It should not be seen as inferior to the long-term efforts to communicate with mutual understanding and goodwill which is the basis for a good relationship and which provides the accurate information upon which sensible and humane decisions can be made.

Communicating with the mentally infirm

The approaches and pitfalls already considered apply equally to mentally infirm elderly people. There is an even greater need to respect these vulnerable personalities which, with some exceptions, may be more at the mercy of officialdom than at any time since childhood. This does not mean that social workers accept everything a mentally disturbed person says as an accurate account of reality. They should be alert to signs of hallucinations or delusions. They should listen to a confused old person with the same close attention as they would to a rational person, noting inconsistencies and discrepancies in their account of events. They should recognize that confused old people sometimes give accurate information and that relatives and neighbours sometimes depart from the truth.

A special kind of listening skill needs to be cultivated when communicating with mentally infirm people. Social workers need to sustain attention and to relate what is heard to what is already known about the old person's history and situation. They should speak when the old person reaches a phase of lucidity as this is the point at which what is said is most likely to be accepted and understood. They should remember one of the sad lessons of the Maria Colwell case. Nobody listened to what Maria said, nor recognized the significance of what she did. There is an equal danger that nobody will listen to what mentally infirm elderly people say, or give it due weight before decisions are taken. It is equally vital that the old person should be kept informed about the state of her own health, what help is available, and what the caring services are trying to do on her behalf.

COMMUNICATING WHEN THE CLIENT IS AGITATED OR CONFUSED

Sometimes social workers arrive at an old person's home when she is in a very agitated or confused state. It does not help to speak sharply or to argue with her at such a time. Distraction is the best soother. If the confused old lady sets off in her pinafore to walk the hundred or so miles which separate her from her daughter, she might be asked, 'Can I come too?' She may walk as far as the bus stop or to the corner shop. The original intention is often quickly forgotten and the suggestion may be put, 'It is rather a cold day, shall we go back home and get our coats?' In this way the return home can be achieved without distress or harm, and without reinforcing the old person's delusions. Arguments, or attempts to restrain, tend to increase agitation and confusion.

REDUCING AGITATION

It is sometimes possible to encourage a more lucid interval, if the old person's conversation continues to be disorientated and deluded, by talking about an earlier, happier period in her life. Previous knowledge of the old lady will help the decision whether to mention a husband, a son, a daughter, a sister, a brother, or even a job, as a topic which will provoke a positive response. In other instances, a photograph may provide a useful focus for conversation.

The approach to agitated old people is very similar to that of a loving and imaginative mother to an overwrought child. She patiently presents pleasing and soothing alternatives to activities which she cannot condone. The difference is that a parent expects to use her skill in this way, whereas relatives, neighbours, friends, even members of the caring professions, may be disconcerted to have to do so in dealing with elderly people. They may begin by reacting angrily, and by telling the old person not to be silly. This only increases tension; a quiet, patient approach tends to reduce pressure and to shorten periods of distress. Social workers should react calmly to irrational behaviour and respond warmly to periods of lucidity.

The nurse best able to help acutely disturbed schizophrenic patients in 'I Never Promised you a Rose Garden' (Green 1972), was a strong, well-balanced man. He wanted his patients to be like himself. 'He kept calling attention to the similarity between them ... and when a scrap came forth, he welcomed it.' The doctor best able to help tried to deal honestly with her patients, telling them what they could achieve, but not holding out false hopes or false promises.

Summary

Old people can be communicated with orally, by letter, or by non-verbal means. Due consideration should be paid when speaking with an old person to a possible deterioration in sight, or hearing, or a decline in alertness and concentration. If the elderly person is agitated or deluded she may sometimes be calmed by talking about something pleasant in her past life. It is better to distract her from an irrational plan than to oppose it. Show interest, patience, and warmth of response. Guidelines for communication are included in Appendix 4(c), pp.182–3.

10 SOCIAL WORK INTERVENTION

Lord thou knowest better than I know myself that I am growing older and will some day be old. Keep me from the fatal habit of thinking I must say something on every subject and on every occasion. Release me from craving to straighten out everybody's affairs. Make me thoughtful but not moody: helpful but not bossy. With my vast store of wisdom, it seems a pity not to use it all, but Thou knowest Lord that I want a few friends at the end. (Based on a seventeenth-century nun's prayer: source unknown.)

Introduction
This chapter has four aims.

First, to give some guidance to social workers who are asked to make an assessment of an old person who is acting in a peculiar or bizarre fashion and has been the subject of a referral (see Appendix 4(b), pp.175–82). It is not intended to analyse general interview techniques which have been discussed in other publications (see Schweinitz (1962); Rich (1968); Benjamin (1969); Kadushin (1972); Garrett (1972); Cross (1974)).

Second, to consider ways in which social workers, doctors, and other members of the health services can co-operate to help sick old people.

Third, to consider some way of dealing with problem situations which social workers have to face in supporting elderly people in their own homes or in residential homes or hospitals, or, as a last resort, in taking action by a court order to remove them from their own homes, or arranging compulsory admission to hospital.

Fourth, to demonstrate that work with elderly people demands

112

just as much professional skill and use of social work resources as would be involved with the most exacting and under-privileged younger clients (see Goldberg 1970: 197).

Referrals – How are they recognized

Old people tend not to ask for help for themselves, so that their needs have to be recognized by others (see Cole and Utting (1962); Townsend and Wedderburn (1965); Abel-Smith and Townsend 1965)). Referrals come from various sources including the family doctor, a hospital doctor, health visitor, police officer, home help or voluntary worker, a neighbour, a relative, or a friend.

In order to get help to old people at an early stage in their illness, it is necessary for an informed and knowledgeable person, such as an ancillary health worker or a volunteer, to alert the appropriate service. An alternative is to encourage members of the public in close touch with an elderly person to report signs of deterioration to their area social work or hospital-based team. A third way is to compile a register of elderly people in need of various social services and to screen at regular intervals the most vulnerable groups (see p.90). A fourth approach is for group practices regularly to check old people on their lists. Singly or together these four procedures should provide a useful early warning system.

Non-medical referrals

The most common non-medical referral comes from a close relative or a neighbour of the elderly patient. In all such instances a social worker with the consent of the old person, if she is not too ill to understand, should get in touch with the local doctor telling him of the situation and asking for relevant information about the patient. Such a contact may already have been made by the relative; if so the social worker will confirm with the GP that she is actively involved with the patient, and will ask for information about the illness and its implication. If the GP is not available for consultation a community nurse or health visitor attached to the practice may be able to help. The person referring the old lady to the Social Service Department should normally be kept informed of the efforts which are being made. In some instances he or she may be able either to initiate or to give the social worker useful support in her enquiries.

Some underlying assumptions

Social workers tend to assume that wherever they can marshal appropriate support and services their first aim should be to keep old people living either in their own home or with relatives or friends. This may involve giving a great deal of practical help and counselling support to the relatives as well as directly to the elderly person. This aim is generally a useful one but in the case of mentally infirm old people, their abnormal behaviour, even when conditioned by social and psychological factors, is nearly always caused, aggravated, or accompanied by disease. Until this disease has been identified, evaluated, and treated, the cause and outcome of the mental abnormality is obscure. An informed medical opinion should therefore be the social worker's first aim if her intervention is to be helpful and effective.

Medical diagnosis and prognosis – the GP and the social worker

As long as elderly people are living in their own homes or in another private household, their local doctor has ultimate responsibility for their physical and mental well-being. The GP either on the basis of his own examination or after consultation with a geriatrician or psychiatrist, will be able to tell the social worker what he believes to be the medical cause of the patient's abnormal behaviour. He may also be able to indicate how long the disturbance may last, whether or not it is irreversible, what treatment or specialist help may be needed, and, in some instances, how long the patient may survive.

The social worker needs this basic information in order to make effective plans, to advise those nursing the invalid and to help them to cope with their anxiety. Different help may be necessary for a patient suffering from extrinsic brain failure (acute confusional state) who has recently become ill, from one suffering from non-vascular intrinsic brain failure (senile dementia) where the decline has been slow and insidious (see pp.10–13). The former may be speedily restored to normality, the latter is likely to need long-term support.

Co-operation is a two-way process

The doctor's medical advice is crucial to the success of social work support. Equally the knowledge which a social worker may have about an infirm person's background, previous standards, and

114

behaviour, may be of considerable significance for the doctor. He may also welcome information about available social aids and services. It will be greatly to the patient's advantage if workers from both disciplines can spare the time to get to know each other personally. They will not always be able to discuss each case face-to-face, but they will be able to maintain their relationship by consulting on the telephone or by means of letters. As both will be seeking to further the best interests of the patient, both may need to overcome barriers erected for self-protection. The doctor's receptionist and the social worker's office staff should be encouraged to convey clear messages. Future co-operation is likely to depend on effective mutual help in the past.

Relationship with hospital consultants
Social workers may receive referrals directly from a geriatrician or a psychiatrist who will already have detailed medical information about a patient. Unlike the GP, they are unlikely to be familiar with her home situation and family circumstances. For this reason they will welcome a social work report which gives certain basic information. This includes data about the old person's behaviour before the onset of the present illness. They will want to know whether her housing, living conditions, household conditions, or the state of her home have declined or changed recently. They will be interested in how far the old person is able to care for herself and whether she can call upon help from a friend, neighbour, or relative. Are her relatives prepared to help, able to cope with the illness, and do they understand its nature? They will want to know what aids and services have been available to the elderly person and what further help could be marshalled on her behalf (see Appendix 4(b), pp.176–82 for assessment form). Consultants will welcome reports of any changes in the situation or state of health of the patient after discharge from a geriatric unit or hospital. When necessary, further medical treatment can be arranged with the purpose of restoring the patient's ability to care for herself.

The social worker, like the geriatrician and the psychiatrist, will only want people to leave their homes for the shortest possible time while appropriate treatment is given. Pressure on hospital beds and a recognition that old people are more contented and less confused in a familiar environment will serve to unite the social work and medical team in their joint efforts.

As in the case of the GP there is a great advantage in hospital

115

consultants having an opportunity to meet area social workers. They will welcome a brief note including the social worker's name, address, and telephone number and the fact that she is currently helping the patient. Free exchange of information between health and social work staff can only be to the advantage of the elderly person.

Initial assessment of the patient

Only in an emergency situation should social work assessments be made on the basis of one interview. The pace of the old is slow and should not be forced.

A social worker normally sees the old person in her own home where her family circumstances may offer useful clues to the nature of the problem (see Appendix 7, pp.190–5). Occasionally she does not want to be seen in her own home and her wishes must be respected. The social worker may find out whether the patient has recently moved into the area and has suddenly begun to neglect herself and her home. She can see whether the old lady has food and means of keeping herself warm and properly nourished. She can note whether the door is locked and barred, sealed with sellotape, or left on the latch. She can find out whether the old lady has recently suffered any loss, bereavement, or change in circumstance which may have adversely affected her. She will not normally be concerned with the old person's actual standard of home comfort, but with any sudden change in it which cannot adequately be explained. The social worker's intention will be to try and build up a picture of the kind of person this old lady has been and the kind of person she has become (see assessment form, Appendix 4(b), pp.176–82).

Arrangements for the interview

The social worker cannot always organize the interview as she would wish. Wherever possible she should do her best to talk with the old person and with any relatives both separately and together. She can then compare the various accounts of events which are given as well as assess the atmosphere which the old person's illness has engendered. Relatives should be seen on their own if the patient will allow this. If she is too suspicious to make this easy, a separate appointment should be made.

Interviewing relatives, friends, and neighbours
Those living with or near to a disturbed elderly person will be able
to give their first-hand account of her mental state and situation.
Their version should never be asked for without the consent of the
patient unless she is too disturbed to understand the nature of the
request.

Relatives and others may be agitated and anxious when they give
their account of events. They may distort the picture either
deliberately because they are desperate for help, or unintentionally
because they are distressed. The neighbour who begins by insisting
'Something must be done', may be at the end of her tether and
may concentrate on the most recent outrage in the patient's mental
history. The social worker needs to reassure relatives that she has
come to the house in order to try to do something, but that she
cannot make up her mind what is the most appropriate action until
she has a fuller picture of the position. She needs to convey by her
attitude that she takes their complaints seriously and that she is
listening to them with concern, but that she must take more than
one view into account. There must be a clear commitment that
support will be given; otherwise relatives are unlikely to be
co-operative.

Those caring for an elderly person who is deteriorating rapidly
may suffer a great deal themselves. Feelings of shame, guilt, and
distress may overwhelm them and make them initially disturbed
and poor witnesses. They may begin by speaking in a distraught
and angry fashion but if they are given an opportunity to unburden
themselves to a sympathetic person, their account of events will
soon become more balanced. They should be treated with patience
and respect so that their confidence will be won and they will be
able to relax and give an accurate and detailed account of events.
The social worker's main purpose in the initial interview is to obtain
information. The way in which she does this may give many
opportunities to reassure her informants, and so indirectly to treat
both the situation and the disturbed old person.

Interviewing the old person
Social workers normally try to listen with patience and respect to
everything a client has to say. In addition, they try to avoid
distorting what is being said to them by the nature of their response
or by asking leading questions. In no group is this more important
than in the elderly with mental infirmity. The questions phrased by

117

the interviewer should not lead to a 'yes' or 'no' answer but should always be 'open-ended'. For example, one would never say to a patient, 'Did you get up at two o'clock this morning and knock at the neighbour's door?' Instead the approach would be along the lines, 'What sort of night did you have last night?' or 'Were you disturbed in any way?' (See also pp.28, and 109–10.)

Reliability of evidence

Chapter 3 and Chapter 4 give an account of behaviour which is characteristic of those suffering from brain failure and from the affective psychoses and paraphrenia. (See in particular pp.22–6, 32–4, and 37–9.) The evidence of such people may for a variety of reasons be untrustworthy and difficult to elicit.

The social worker needs to be aware of the range of behaviour which those suffering from mental infirmity may display. She should recognize that the old person's state of mind distorts her ability to give an accurate account of recent events and her own actions. On the other hand, she should be on her guard against devaluing all they say. Even the most disturbed old lady will speak the truth on some occasions, and even the most truthful relative may mislead under the stress of strong emotion. The social worker should take due note of the reliability and character of those giving information and their interest in the outcome of the enquiry.

Initial action

After the initial interview or interviews the social worker should prepare a short report to convey to the family doctor or to any other referring agency, with her recommendations.

The social worker has not only synthesized information from various sources, but she has also initiated a relationship with the patient and with those surrounding her and gained insight into their behaviour and motives.

Containing the situation

She has also established her identity and a link with the family for the future. Very often nothing more than this can be done at this time. This is one of the more important things for social workers to learn. When, as is quite often the case in early brain failure, a person is wandering at night but appears mentally normal by day, and when there is no evidence of physical illness or malnutrition, she may resist suggestions to attend hospitals, out-patient departments, day hospitals, or day centres. She will probably refuse drugs and see no need for any of the measures proposed. Her neighbours and friends, partly to relieve their own anxiety, may press for such help to be given. The social worker needs to listen patiently to their views and try to help them to understand that such services will be of little use to a resistant, mentally infirm person. Rather than solve a problem it may only transfer it to a different location.

Sometimes all that the social worker and the neighbours can do is to accept what the old person wants and to wait for something drastic to happen when action will be appropriate. Meanwhile the situation has changed significantly. The social worker and the doctor know of the old person's condition. Both will keep an eye on the situation. They will listen to any further complaints of neighbours, help to reduce their high level of anxiety, and suggest the appropriate time for intervention. This is not doing nothing; it is doing something extremely valuable.

The social worker as a resource person

This does not mean that practical help cannot be given. Services which may be useful have been described in Chapter 8. The social worker should use her skill as an enabler to help old people to accept the services they need. Frequently she will seek to collaborate with other statutory and voluntary agencies, acting as co-ordinator and seeking to ensure that the services function smoothly and appropriately. Help directed to the family and to concerned friends may indirectly improve the lot of the old person herself (see Chapter 11). In other instances, the social worker will be concerned to discover and to keep contact with caring people who will give affection and support to the vulnerable old person. Such people will also be able to report any deterioration in the old person's condition. Some interpretations and possible solutions to a variety of problems faced by an elderly mentally infirm old lady are recorded in Appendix 7, pp.190–5.

Long-term plans

RESIDENTIAL ACCOMMODATION
Bumagin has pointed out that the obvious solution, such as the availability of a place in an old people's home, is not always the best (see Dr Hazelhurst's suggestion, Appendix 7, p.190). A hostile, suspicious old person might be better served by a group

of community helpers in her own home rather than risk antagonism
and the wearing out of her welcome in a residential home (Bumagin
1972). A difficult personality can be endured for short periods,
but may over the long term drain the resources of residential staff
and residents alike. Normally the social worker should not suggest
a place in a Home. Unless the proposal is initiated by the old person,
it may well cause her anxiety and may lead to a further decline
in her mental health. However, if the proposal is made, the
consequences should be discussed in detail. Ideally, the old person
should be encouraged to visit the Home and to get first-hand
experience of living there before making a final decision.

A 'FLOATING BED' ARRANGEMENT

At times the situation can be helped (and in some instances the
carers relieved) if the old person is given short-term treatment in
hospital for her illness, restored to her home, and re-admitted for
treatment if her condition deteriorates. (Some hospitals admit on a
sliding scale from one week in, six out, to one week in, three out.)
Such a situation requires tactful handling. The old person should
be prepared for what is going to happen. Meacher has described the
awful bewilderment of old people who end up in hospital or a
Home after 'being taken for a ride' (Meacher 1972).

TEAM WORK ON DISCHARGE

Discharge also needs to be well handled. This will involve careful
collaboration between consultants, nursing staff, and hospital and
area social workers. If one link in this chain breaks, an old person
who has responded well to treatment may deteriorate in a few hours.
An old lady in her eighties was sent back to an empty house. There
was no proper means of conveying her from the ambulance into
her sitting room. She was dumped unceremoniously on to a chair
and left overnight without food or the means of going to the
lavatory. When the social worker arrived the next day she found her
in great distress and discomfort (see also pp.143–4).

Cleaning and repairing a neglected home

Sometimes a temporary admission to hospital gives social workers
and members of the family an opportunity to clean up a dirty house
and make repairs to the property. This should be done only with
the free consent and approval of the owner, otherwise what is meant
to be helpful may have very unfortunate repercussions. A woman

of 85 who was nearly ready for discharge from hospital was told that she could not go home until she had agreed to have her house thoroughly cleaned. Under these circumstances she agreed. When she returned home, she discovered that all the neighbours knew what had happened because an official van had stood outside her house for several days and some of her furniture had been burned in the garden. She was distressed because an old three-legged stool which she had used 'to kill the pigs on' and a broken umbrella which had belonged to her mother had been thrown away – the former because it was unsafe and the latter because it was of no practical use. To her these articles represented irreplaceable memories of her past life. Because of this experience she was angry with her relatives who had allowed it to happen and resolved never to open her door again to 'one of those welfare people'.

Avoid over-protection
Sometimes an excess of concern can be to the detriment of an old person. A women in her eighties whose health and strength were failing, found herself surrounded by strange people all anxious to give her help but oblivious of her need for privacy and quiet. She was heard to say, 'Far too many people have the key to my house.' Barnes, Sack, and Shore (1973) offer a simple diagram (*Figure 3*) which seeks to show the way in which social attitudes and well-meaning efforts to help an elderly person can undermine first their confidence and independence and ultimately their mental health. Dependent people can be the victim of indiscriminate efforts to protect and help them. They may be kept safe at the cost of all that gives savour to living and sometimes at the sacrifice of their dignity and privacy. Elderly people like anyone else should be allowed to take some risks.

Avoiding premature disengagement
At one extreme there is the danger of officiousness and over-protection, at the other there is danger of disengaging too soon. If an old person goes into a hospital or Home, she will continue to need to keep in touch with her local social worker. The latter should offer support and comfort during the early days of a transition which would challenge even a healthy and well-balanced person. She should seek to preserve the link between the old person and her family and friends at home. She should collaborate with residential or hospital staff sharing with them her special

121

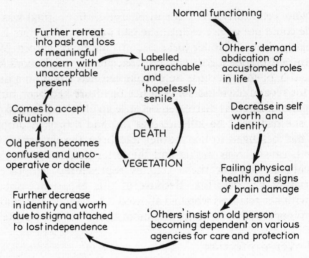

Figure 3 *Cycle of dementia*

Adapted from Barnes, Sack, and Shore (1973). Reprinted by permission of *The Gerontologist*.

knowledge of her client. She should avoid looking upon a long-term placement as the resolution of the problem. The old person is no longer at risk and her health and safety are being cared for. Nevertheless the social worker is an irreplaceable link with the past. She is a key person, particularly in the absence or remoteness of relatives and friends, in renewing what Ruth Cohen calls the old person's need to be 'not cared for, but cared about' (Cohen 1957).

Crisis intervention (1)

REMOVAL FROM HOME

Section 47 of the National Assistance Act, 1948, gives the medical authorities power to arrange for the removal of persons needing care and attention who are:

(i) suffering from grave chronic disease, or being aged, infirm, or physically incapacitated, are living in insanitary conditions;

(ii) unable to devote to themselves, and are not receiving from other persons, proper care and attention (see Appendix 1, p.165).

Since the reorganization of the Social Service Departments, requests for compulsory removal of old people from their homes have increased.

These are difficult decisions to take. Those involved have to decide what constitutes 'grave chronic disease' and what 'insanitary conditions'. They must also be concerned about what 'proper care and attention' involves. They need to consider each individual's unique circumstances. On what criteria do they make their decision? How do they measure the sometimes conflicting demands of the protection of society and the rights of the individual to as much freedom as possible?

MRS HANNAH CHADWICK, AGED 88

Mrs Chadwick is a client in such a critical situation. She lives alone in her own house and was taken to hospital four years ago when her doctor found her lying on the floor after a minor stroke. At this time she was already known to her local health visitor. Her friend, Mrs Pickford, who had lived next door for over forty years, shopped for her and 'kept an eye on her'.

After three months Mrs Chadwick was transferred to a geriatric hospital. She was anxious to return home. She was taken on a short home visit by her hospital occupational therapist to see if she could manage on her own. At this time she was fit only to dress herself and to move with the help of a zimmer frame.

Her home was filthy and neglected. The garden was completely overgrown. There were steep steps up to the front door. The sink was cluttered and the taps rusty. Moths and mice had infested the house. Upstairs (which Mrs Chadwick could only reach with great difficulty) the toilet seat was plastered with faeces and the cistern would not flush. Using the outside WC involved a hazardous journey for an old lady.

The Social Service Department was notified of Mrs Chadwick's predicament. After discussion with her, Mrs Pickford, and the hospital doctor, it was suggested the Mrs Chadwick should go into a Home. She refused this but withdrew her opposition to having her property cleaned. She also agreed to accept domiciliary services and to attend the hospital day centre. She wanted the WC put into working order but doubted if she could afford it. She was provisionally discharged home six months after her stroke. Mrs Pickford tried to air her house and to buy her some food but was not pleased about the discharge. In her view the hospital would have to take responsibility for any consequences.

Mrs Chadwick was sustained by her neighbour for several weeks, after which the situation began to worsen. A neighbourhood petition was organized complaining about the state of her house and garden. Mrs Chadwick remained cheerful but became increasingly unsteady and fell several times. She left full milk bottles outside and vegetables rotting in the hall. She refused all domiciliary services and after several weeks stopped attending the hospital day centre and would not open her door to the ambulance men. Her neighbour continued to call in daily. A hospital-based social worker began to visit the old lady at this time. She found her shaky and tired. She seemed to be 'using the fireplace for a toilet'. Her neighbour was unable to continue to visit daily because her own husband was taken seriously ill. The social worker therefore visited regularly over the next few months. Mrs Chadwick did not appear to be eating much. Her health was poor but she was mobile enough to collect her own pension book. She still refused day care. At this juncture, the hospital staff suggested applying for a Section 47 order. No action was taken.

The social worker continued to call for another twelve months. During this time Mrs Chadwick had several falls, she appeared confused at times, and her house and sanitary conditions deteriorated. Neighbours again complained about the state of her home and garden. The old lady remained cheerful. She talked coherently about events in her past life going back to 1916. The health visitor began to visit her regularly again and the hospital social worker withdrew.

A year later Mrs Chadwick, after repeated falls, was seen at the outpatient clinic at the hospital. She was not admitted but the hospital social worker was told of her condition. She began to visit again and succeeded, with the old lady's consent, in arranging for the delivery of meals at home twice a week and for a home help to call. Within three days Mrs Chadwick had fallen again. She was admitted to hospital suffering from bad bruising and lacerations. She was in a filthy condition and incontinent. Her neighbour asked if she could be placed into institutional care. Mrs Pickford had been visiting three times a day. She was finding this increasingly burdensome as her own elderly mother was now living with her. Mrs Chadwick steadfastly refused to go into a Home and was again discharged home with full support services including a community nurse and laundry service. At present, she is still living in her own home. Is this justifiable, or should Mrs Chadwick have been removed at this point or earlier under a Section 47 order?

CRITERIA FOR DECISION

The problem is how to give the individual as much freedom as possible in such a situation as this. The decision would have been simpler if Mrs Chadwick had been suffering from brain failure and had allowed her housekeeping and self-care to decline as a consequence. This was not so. Mrs Chadwick is, and has been for at least the last forty years, a solitary, eccentric individual with very low housekeeping standards. Are the medical authorities justified in intervening in her life in order to improve her conditions? Her house and garden, though appalling, are quite separate from her neighbours. Do the claims of the neighbours, particularly that of Mrs Pickford, outweigh that of the old person, and if so at what point? Do Mrs Chadwick's insanitary habits, which cause offence rather than harm to others, justify limiting her freedom against her will?

A medical examination with prognosis is a vital part of making such a decision. But if the prognosis is poor, removal from home could add mental confusion to organic injury and disease and would have caused a further decline in Mrs Chadwick's state. What if medical treatment is refused? Does this justify compulsory removal in her case? Should action be taken solely on the grounds that harm may be done to others? Or in her case when does a calculated risk become an unjustified risk? The responsibility should only be taken away from an old person if she is not capable of decision making or is endangering the lives of others.

One factor which may be taken into consideration is whether the squalor predated the decline. In such a case the worker's own standards of home care, or reference to a mythical average standard, are not relevant. Another important consideration is whether, after treatment and convalescence combined with practical help, the old person may be better able to manage her affairs. If the prognosis is hopeless should she be allowed to run the risk of dying alone in her own home or should she be taken into hospital where she may lie in a long-stay hospital ward for months or even years? (see p.22). There are no solutions which fit all cases. The problem of authority and individual freedom raises many difficult ethical questions which cannot be ignored. Intervening in the life of another for her own good can be inimical to individual freedom. It is in this area that old people are particularly vulnerable (see Appendix 4(b), pp.175–6).

Crisis intervention (2)

COMPULSORY ADMISSION TO HOSPITAL

Where psychiatric treatment is required on an in-patient basis the majority of patients enter hospital voluntarily. The GP and the social worker will go to considerable trouble to try to ensure that this is so, encouraging and persuading reluctant individuals to accept the medical treatment offered. In certain rare instances persuasion fails and it appears that treatment is essential in the interests of the old person's health or her safety, or in order to protect others from possible injury. In such circumstances the Mental Health Act, 1959, lays down various procedures for compulsory admission to hospital (see Appendix 1, pp.167–8). When is it necessary to take such drastic action and under what section of the Act? Consider the case of Mrs Sennett.

MRS VERA SENNETT, AGED 75

Mrs Sennett, a widow, lives alone in a local authority old person's flat. Below her lives another elderly lady, Mrs West, whose husband has recently died.

Three years ago Mrs West approached the social worker at her local Health Centre complaining that Mrs Sennett had begun to bang on her door between 1.00 a.m. and 4.30 a.m. The problem had been going on for several months. The banging occurred two or three times a night, interspersed with periods of relative quiet.

The social worker visited Mrs Sennett. She found a short plump woman with a wild look in her eyes wearing poor, untidy clothes. Her flat was cold and cluttered, presenting a considerable contrast to Mrs West's comfortable home below. Nevertheless, Mrs Sennett spoke rationally and sensibly most of the time and exhibited no bizarre characteristics.

The social worker set out to contain the situation by visiting Mrs Sennett with the object of giving her interest and support and by visiting Mrs West with the aim of helping her to endure the situation and possibly to gain insight into her neighbour's mental state. She also offered to help Mrs West to apply for a transfer to another flat. This practical solution failed because Mrs West did not like the alternative accommodation offered. She did not want to leave her immediate neighbours. They preferred that Mrs Sennett should be the one to move.

There were no other outbreaks of banging for nearly a year, but then two further incidents caused Mrs West to return to the Health Centre to renew her complaints. On these two occasions Mrs Sennett was not only troublesome at night, she also followed Mrs West along the footpath during the daytime threatening to kill her.

The social worker called on Mrs Sennett and also asked the GP to pay a visit. He agreed to do so promising to give medication to dampen his patient's paranoid ideas. After the second outbreak the social worker was concerned by Mrs Sennett's aggressive reaction to questions. She accused Mrs West of being the troublemaker and of breaking into her flat and of stealing some of her property. Mrs Sennett also claimed to have seen a medium and heard the voice of a neighbour who had recently died. The social worker suggested that Mrs Sennett should see a psychiatrist. She consulted the old lady's GP and he made the necessary arrangements. Both the social worker and the doctor were of the opinion that Mrs Sennett would need in-patient hospital treatment. However, the psychiatrist (an approved officer under the 1959 Act) considered that the old lady was not sufficiently ill to justify a compulsory admission to hospital.

The social worker continued to visit both old ladies regularly – seeing Mrs Sennett once a week. She also negotiated a housing transfer to a different area for Mrs Sennett, who appeared interested and acquiescent until a flat was offered to her, when she rejected it. Why should she move when Mrs West was the aggressor? The social worker was aware that transferring either lady was not a solution to this problem, but she hoped to reduce the anxiety endured by Mrs West, especially if this could be done without causing a deterioration in Mrs Sennett's condition. A month after Mrs Sennett had refused the housing transfer, the tenants of adjoining flats combined to complain of her noisy peram-bulations during the previous night which had continued until 6.40 a.m. She had banged on doors and windows, shouted threats through Mrs West's door and hit it with a blunt instrument. She had also tried to prise open the door with a knife.

A Section 25 admission
When visited by the social worker, Mrs Sennett accused Mrs West of murdering her husband. The social worker was concerned by the

127

violent attack on Mrs West's door and by the generally aggressive nature of Mrs Sennett's ideas and behaviour. She immediately contacted Mrs Sennett's GP who arranged for her to be seen by a psychiatrist. On this occasion, the psychiatrist was of the opinion that Mrs Sennett was sufficiently disturbed to require in-patient hospital treatment. She was suffering from florid paraphrenia. Mrs Sennett rejected efforts to persuade her to go to hospital on a voluntary basis. She did not recognize that she had any need for medical help. She was, therefore, taken to hospital under Section 25 of the 1959 Mental Health Act, where she was detained for observation for twenty-eight days.

After discharge from hospital the community nurse called weekly to give her an injection. This medication effectively reduced Mrs Sennett's paranoid symptoms. The social worker called on her regularly to make sure that she was physically well and properly fed. She noted with regret that Mrs Sennett no longer trusted her. This is one of the reasons that compulsory admissions to hospital should always be a last resort. In Mrs Sennett's case the social worker persevered with indifferent success for many months to re-establish mutual trust.

Ten months after discharge from hospital, Mrs Sennett began again in the small hours to bang on her neighbour's front door. She followed Mrs West when she left her flat threatening to kill her. On several occasions she even accompanied her to the Health Centre where Mrs West, in a very agitated condition, arrived to report the threats.

The social worker tried to call on Mrs Sennett on many occasions but the old lady refused to answer the door. Fortunately, a new GP was appointed to the clinic and Mrs Sennett became his patient. She trusted him and he was able to gain access to her home. He gave her an appointment at the Health Centre and invited the social worker to be present. Together they tried to persuade Mrs Sennett to go voluntarily into hospital for treatment. The old lady was docile and friendly until the hospital was mentioned when she sprang up shouting, 'I'd rather die than go back there!' The social worker and the doctor could neither soothe nor restrain her.

Later, though she again denied access to the social worker, she allowed her GP to visit her. Again, she refused to visit a psychiatrist or to consider in-patient treatment. Her manner was disturbed, her eyes wild, and her speech aggressive. She said she was going to kill her neighbour with a hatchet. The doctor had discovered that she was no longer taking her medication and was unwilling to recommence it. Both he and the social worker considered that Mrs Sennett needed medical treatment; both would have preferred her to receive it either voluntarily or, at worst, under Section 25 of the 1959 Act again. This was impossible because the old lady refused to see a psychiatrist.

A Section 29 admission

The only way in which she could be admitted for hospital treatment therefore was under Section 29 of the Act. This section allows an emergency application to be made by one doctor only (in this case the GP) to admit a patient to hospital and to detain her for observation for up to three days (see Appendix 1, p.168). It is normally reserved for extreme cases only in which great violence either to the patient or to others is likely to be involved.

A further difficulty which had to be overcome was how to transport Mrs Sennett to hospital as there was an ambulance strike. The social worker waited a short time until this was over. She then asked the GP to call on his patient with her. The doctor signed the prescribed forms and left on his rounds. The social worker remained behind with a social work assistant for an unnerving hour and a half waiting for the arrival of the ambulance. When it did turn up, it took the combined efforts of three men to get one small woman into it.

Such a situation is agitating enough for all concerned. The alternative, if the ambulance had been prevented from calling, would have been worse. This would have been to call the police and ask them to take Mrs Sennett to hospital. Neither the police nor the social worker would have welcomed such a desperate solution which would have undoubtedly caused even more distress and damaging public comment.

Section 30 'admission'

Mrs Sennett was admitted to hospital in the first place on an emergency application which lasted for three days. The period was extended for a further three days under Section 30 of the Act so that Mrs Sennett could be examined by a psychiatrist and plans could be made for her effective treatment (see BASW 1977). Subsequently she remained in hospital for twenty-eight days on a Section 25 committal. At the end of this period she agreed to continue in-patient treatment on a voluntary basis. Her social worker was very relieved by this decision.

Section 26 detention for medical treatment

Had Mrs Sennett been unwilling to continue in hospital, it would have been possible to detain her on proper medical grounds for up to a year under Section 26 of the Act (see Appendix 1, p.168). This would not necessarily have meant that she would have remained in hospital for the full period. She could have been allowed home subject to recall for further in-patient treatment if her health broke down again. During the year in which Section 26 was in force Mrs Sennett could have been returned to hospital without the need for further medical reports or for the renewed signature from a social worker. Such powers, which drastically limit the freedom of the individual, are only undertaken when no other solution appears possible.

Criteria for decision

The problem of applying for compulsory admission to hospital is as challenging as that of compulsory removal from home and raises similar ethical issues. The power should be used only with the greatest circumspection.

Decisions should be based on the fullest possible information about the patient's unique circumstances. In all but the rarest instances, a social worker should consult her case records or that of her colleagues if she has to deal with someone unknown to her. Otherwise there is a danger that an absent colleague may have established a close working relationship with the disturbed person and may find her long-term treatment plan upset by action initiated by a less well-informed social worker. Decisions with such grave effects on the liberty of another person invariably should be based on sound knowledge both of her and of her circumstances.

It is not sufficient for a person to be mentally ill to warrant compulsory admission to hospital. An individual has the right to refuse psychiatric treatment (BASW 1977). There are many mentally disturbed old people functioning adequately in the community. Compulsory admission is only appropriate when the refusal to accept medical treatment stems from the nature of the mental illness which is depriving the patient of insight into her condition and of her need for treatment. Further, it is only justified in these circumstances if the old person is likely to do harm to herself or to others. Judging whether this is so, is a skilled task.

Mrs Sennett, like Mrs Chadwick, arouses anxiety and uncertainty; neither woman can be considered in isolation for each is affecting other people's lives. For over three years, Mrs West has at intervals suffered loss of sleep, anxiety, or fear because of her neighbour's behaviour. In her flat she lives in a perpetual state of siege – an experience which her two married daughters claim has adversely affected her health and peace of mind. The social worker strives to reduce her suffering. She is prepared, subject to medical advice, to intervene to protect Mrs West from a possible physical attack. At the same time, she tried to shield Mrs Sennett from an unnecessary loss of liberty.

Reluctance to use compulsory powers arises not only from respect for individual liberty and for self-determination, but also a recognition that compulsory admission to hospital may lead to a deterioration in the patient's attitudes, particularly to those who signed the prescribed form. Normally this is a relative or a social worker (see Appendix 1, pp.166–7). Social workers prefer to sign the form because they are prepared to endure the patient's subsequent hostility or distrust. Relatives may find this antagonism very hard to bear. Whoever signs the form is likely to find her ability to give help is adversely affected, yet this help may be crucial to the old person if she is to function in the community. As a result, the patient, on her return home, is in danger of being even more vulnerable than before treatment.

Social workers, like doctors, prefer voluntary medical treatment. If this is refused, they prefer to invoke a section with a limited period of hospital admission rather than a prolonged one (compare Section 25 and Section 26) and one where two doctors' diagnoses are involved rather than one (compare Section 25 and Section 29). Early discharge tends to prevent both a deterioration in the old person's home circumstances and the possibility of her becoming institutionalized. The danger of long-term compulsory admission is that it may become self-perpetuating.

Summary
This chapter offers some guidance on how a social worker can make an assessment of a mentally disturbed old person. It discusses short-term and long-term plans to give support in collaboration with colleagues from statutory and voluntary services and from the

health services. Removal from home under a court order and compulsory admission to hospital are considered with special reference to the moral issues involved. Case studies and an assessment form are offered for discussion and as aids to learning.

11 NEEDS OF RELATIVES

The extent of the problem
In the early 1970s the number of mentally infirm elderly people living in the community was assessed at between 200,000 and 450,000 according to whether they were suffering from mild or extreme forms of their disability (Meacher 1972: 427–8). This does not represent the full incidence, for old people are poor self-reporters, relatives are often reluctant to ask for medical care, and doctors not always aware that their elderly patients are mentally infirm (Williamson *et al.* 1964; Shanas *et al.* 1968: 87). Evidence suggests that more old people with marked confusion are to be found in private households than in all types of institutions combined (Williamson *et al.* 1964; Kay, Beamish, and Roth 1964). It is not the community that supplements professional efforts to care for the elderly mentally infirm, but the social and health services which try to fill the gaps left by childlessness and isolation or strive to lessen the strain on those who are caring for such individuals within the community (Bayley 1973).

The nature of the problem
The task is made harder by the nature of the problem. Elderly mentally infirm people show reduced capacity to look after themselves, to get about, and to maintain social contacts. They suffer from more disabilities, worse hearing, and poorer eyesight than normal elderly people. They are also more likely to be lonely and isolated, preoccupied with their state of health, self-pitying, and dissatisfied with life. They may show excessive conscientiousness, narrowmindedness, and obstinacy, characteristics which do not make for easy and pleasant social relationships (Kay, Beamish, and

Roth 1964; Post 1944). It is not clear whether these qualities are cause or effect phenomena. Nevertheless they are likely to cause anxiety and unhappiness both to their possessor and to those in contact with her.

Motives for caring

Yet relatives, neighbours, and friends do rally, sometimes at great personal sacrifice, to try to keep the mentally disturbed out of institutional care. They want to avoid seeing the old person either stigmatized or lonely in a strange environment. They feel that the patient will be less distressed, less confused if she remains in a familiar situation (Grad and Sainsbury 1966).

Caring for the mentally infirm is more exacting than nursing a physically sick person. Relatives have to give greater and more unusual kinds of help. They have to come to terms with disorientated behaviour and try to compensate for what is missing in the patient herself. Most of this support is given either by a surviving married partner (twice as frequently the wife rather than the husband) or by an adult child (commonly the daughter), but sisters and brothers as well as more distant relatives, together with neighbours and friends, do upon occasions take on this challenging task. Sometimes a group of people share the responsibility, frequently on a rota basis (Bree 1960). Throughout this chapter the term 'relative' will be used to include friends and neighbours who are acting as 'props' to elderly people in the community. (The term 'prop' is used by Whelan and Bree (1946, 1954).)

The overwhelming motive for giving help is love and affection. Other common motives are loyalty, pride, emotional dependence, or a mixture of these reasons. These attitudes appear to persist over many years and only in a minority of cases does love change to mere loyalty, or loyalty to rejection. Occasionally relatives' own health may fail and reduce their capacity to continue giving support (Bree 1960).

The myth that the welfare state has undermined family responsibility dies hard. The weight of the evidence is that those who are most likely to be admitted to hospital are socially isolated and usually childless (see Sainsbury 1960; Connolly 1962). The neglect of old people by relatives plays a negligible part in demand for hospital admissions (Isaacs 1971). There are some families, and some individuals within otherwise caring families, who do avoid taking on such responsibilities. Rejecting adult children, though rare, tend to be conspicuous and to come to the attention of the Social Service Departments. On the other hand, dutiful, self-sacrificing ones tend to pass unnoticed and to fail to attract attention to their plight until they themselves are old, alone, and in need. (See Miss Grant, Appendix 8, p.196.) Recently the National Council for the Single Woman and her Dependents has drawn public attention to the plight of such women (NCSWD 1973).

Problems faced
How can families willing to care for their elderly mentally infirm best be helped to continue to give support without either under-mining their own physical or mental health or putting their family life in jeopardy? Families appear to be beset by problems arising in three main areas: first, those relating to the behaviour of the elderly relative; second, those due to limitations in their own capacity to do the job; and third, difficulties stemming from doing an exacting task in an unsuitable environment and in some instances to the jeopardy of family harmony (Sanford 1975). (See Appendix 4(d), pp.183–5 for list of problems and some possible solutions.)

(1) BEHAVIOUR OF THE INFIRM PERSON
Loss of sleep
Problems that arise out of the elderly dependent's behaviour are the most difficult to tolerate. Families find loss of sleep particularly trying. Keeping an eye on a confused old person during the day-time is bad enough but it becomes nearly impossible without proper sleep. Relatives describe how the elderly person wanders round the house at night, talking, shouting, or calling repeatedly for help to get on and off the commode. The carers become irritable and touchy. They treat the old person like a naughty child instead of dealing patiently with her. This aggravates an already difficult situation. Sanford (1975) suggests that some children may be bat-tered because their parents are exhausted by lack of sleep. Confused old people can provoke hostility for the same reason. Parents may be concerned if they find their children awakened in the middle of the night by grandmother wandering through their bedrooms. (See Mr and Mrs Redding, Appendix 8, p.196.)

Faecal incontinence
Another cause for complaint is faecal incontinence which, like night wandering, is associated with senile dementia. Unlike urinary

135

incontinence, which is well tolerated, faecal incontinence proves burdensome. It involves frequent and heavy laundering of bed-clothes and personal linen. 'There is the awful smell, too, it goes right through the house', one middle-aged woman said. 'I am ashamed to have anyone come in and I can't relish my food any more.'

Dealing with physical dependence and irresponsibility
A third frequent cause of complaint concerned elderly people who could not, without help, get in or out of bed or on and off the commode. Dangerous irresponsibility in contrast is often endured with surprising patience. Relatives will use great ingenuity to contain the situation. They may turn off the gas at source, lock the outside door, fix guards in front of the fire, install electric fires near to the ceiling, and place safety doors at the top of the stairs. They will often welcome advice on safety factors and find some relief in describing how an elderly relative overcame their best efforts to keep her out of harm. Safety devices may do the opposite of what is intended if they arouse a feverish interest in the sick person. Brenda Kidman in a radio programme called *Where's the Key?* (first broadcast in September 1977) gave a poignant account of her mother's last year of life. She locked the door of their cottage to prevent her mother wandering away and risking exposure and injury on the roads. The result was that her mother followed her around endlessly asking, 'Where's the key?'

Incompatible personalities
Occasionally relatives endure a good deal of strain because their parent's personality is incompatible with their own, or because of her unpredictable bursts of aggression. A mentally infirm person does not always act out of character. Nevertheless the deterioration in her personality may cause great pain to those who love her and remember her earlier vigour. One old man who was looking after his 82-year-old wife said, 'She is a shadow of what she was but she's still kind'. Another family had cared for their 87-year-old father for seven years. He was still strong and vigorous but totally incontinent and disorientated as to time and place. He had always been a self-centred man and was a difficult, demanding invalid. His daughter-in-law was described by her GP as on the edge of a nervous breakdown. She said, 'I feel I am sacrificing my husband and children for a selfish old man I never liked'. Mrs Fairlie,

another old lady who suffered from brain failure, had always dominated her daughter. When the mother became mentally disturbed she showed a bullying attitude to her daughter who complained 'She seems to have taken against me'. With other people Mrs Fairlie never showed overt aggression (see Appendix 8, p.197). Another loving but exhausted family of two sisters and a brother explained that their mother behaved perfectly well when others were present but played them up abominably in private. One of the daughters claimed that her domineering mother had been responsible for the recent breakdown of her marriage.

Multiple problems
Relatives commonly complain of three kinds of behaviour. The first arises when the elderly patient makes excessive demands for help and attention; the second when they constantly describe various physical symptoms; the third when the confused old person is in danger, like Mrs Kidman's mother, of unwittingly doing herself harm. These three characteristics commonly occur in mentally confused people and may combine to make an exceptionally trying situation. It is more common for families to be beset by a variety of problems, (Sanford shows an average of nine per family) than to be overwhelmed by a single intractable one.

Unresponsive behaviour of infirm person
It is not just the variety of demands made on families which undermines them. Another considerable source of strain is the sick person's inability to realize how burdensome they are. They cannot help themselves or try to help those who are nursing them as physically sick people would normally do. They fail to respond and to show in words or with a smile their gratitude for the help given them. They disconcert by their inconsistent behaviour, walking unaided at one moment and shortly afterwards needing support to move from one room to another. They are oblivious of the needs of others, rather like a baby who has not yet recognized that other people have a separate existence. One study of schizophrenics at home showed that relatives were prepared to endure much if they felt emotionally rewarded (Creer and Wing 1974). Unresponsive behaviour acts as a great disincentive to those caring for disturbed old people.

137

(2) LIMITATIONS OF CARERS

Age, fatigue

In many cases (over half according to Sanford), those who look after mentally infirm people are themselves of pensionable age, or as Cresswell (1972) puts it, it is a matter of 'the frail who lead the frail'. Another potential source of breakdown is fatigue due to the length of time that relatives have had to care for their infirm dependants. Nearly three-quarters of one group of elderly people admitted with organic mental symptoms to a geriatric unit had been deteriorating for at least a year and over half for longer than two years (Colwell and Post 1959). There is evidence that certain elderly patients have been cared for in private households for periods of up to fifteen years. Only a minority of the carers had given up the responsibility either because of a breakdown in their own health or because they were disinclined to continue to give support (Bree 1960). Gradually the strength and capacity of either an individual or a whole family can be undermined. The process may be accelerated if the old person also shows the restless energy characteristic of some mentally disturbed people, who are rarely still and apparently never tired.

Prolonged strain

Under such prolonged strain, relatives are not always treated with the consideration they deserve. One gentle, conscientious woman in her early sixties, who had supported her mother for over thirty years, was made to feel like an uncaring daughter by a new social worker unaware of her full circumstances. (See Mrs Celest, Appendix 8, p.197.) Kushlick has pointed out that social workers spend an average of ten minutes a day with a client whereas relatives are on duty for the whole of the twenty-four hours (Kushlick *et al.* 1976). Sometimes even the most conscientious members of the caring staff forget that they do not have to face the long-term, inescapable, and continuous daily demands of dependent elderly people. In such instances, practical services and aids are rarely enough. Relatives need counselling support to enable them to continue to bear the burden or to accept that they have reached a point where others should take over a part or the whole of their responsibilities.

Deterioration in mental health

The mental health of many relatives is affected as a result of the strain they suffer. Some are emotionally disturbed by worrying about the patient, and a few attribute neurotic symptoms such as insomnia, headaches, excessive irritability, and depression to concern about their patient's behaviour (Grad and Sainsbury 1968). They feel that living day in, day out with someone who is withdrawn or unpredictable takes a tremendous toll. They sometimes find that they are reproducing the behaviour of the infirm old person or are infected by their depressed moods. Relatives may be anxious when they are unsure of what is going to happen next, dejected when their efforts to help fail, and guilty if their support is not seen as adequate by neighbours, doctors, or social workers (Creer and Wing 1974). Underlying these reactions is a deeper sense of loss and grief, because they may still get fleeting glimpses of the once healthy personality of the invalid. Small wonder in such circumstances that relatives are sometimes in as great a need of medical and psychiatric help as the original patient.

Physical disabilities and exhaustion

Less frequently physical symptoms like back-ache are attributed to the drudgery of nursing an invalid (Sanford 1975). Complaints are rare considering the high average age of those doing the job. Relatives, particularly elderly spouses, may be near to total exhaustion, yet appear to be resigned to their state until their own collapse precipitates a crisis. Sometimes a perceptive GP keeps a sympathetic eye on the carer and alerts the Social Service Department to the need for support and aid. At other times the doctor may want to help but be unaware of what services are available. In such cases the relatives tend to struggle on unaided.

Caring for parent of opposite sex

Occasionally middle-aged children are embarrassed to have to deal with the intimate toilet of a parent of the opposite sex. Women, more often used to caring for children, appear to overcome initial reluctance more easily than men who may find false delicacy an absolute bar (Sanford 1975). Community nurses, if able to handle the situation with competence and tact, can help adult children to adjust smoothly to this reversal of earlier roles. Otherwise, relatives may be affronted by seeing elderly parents stripped for a bath without consideration for old-fashioned standards of personal modesty;

they may be distressed by this abrupt invasion of privacy which normally their parents would have resented.

Failure to understand the nature of the illness

Both sexes may suffer equally from observing the bizarre behaviour which a deteriorating parent begins to exhibit. It can be seen as deliberate or perverse. When Darius Clayhanger, in Arnold Bennett's novel *Clayhanger* suddenly failed to cut up a sausage on his plate, his son showed him how to do it. 'Edwin put the knife into his right hand and the fork into his left; but in a moment they were wrong again. At first Edwin could not believe that his father was not indulging deliberately in naughtiness. "Shall I cut it up for you, father?" Maggie asked, in a mild persuasive tone.'

Inappropriate ways of trying to help

One compassionate and highly intelligent son, plagued by his father's delusion that he was being denied food, asked the old man to sign a note whenever he received a meal. The son, like Edwin, could not accept that his once outstandingly competent father was simply unable to recall something he had done only a few minutes earlier. Loving relatives may plague themselves and their invalids by asking questions which test memory or require information. 'Tell me what's wrong so that I can help?' repeated Mrs Kidman to her unfortunate mother in *Where's the Key?*. The mother was incapable of doing so. Maggie Clayhanger was wiser. She accepted her father's incapacity and offered unobtrusive assistance. A relative seeking to solve an infirm parent's problems by intellectual means may be frustrated, whereas a nurturing person is likely to contain the situation better, and to torment herself less.

Personal stress and practical tasks

Adult children may be disconcerted by witnessing irrational behaviour, not only because of the nature of the acts, but also because they are afraid that they, in later life, may develop similar characteristics. 'The parent seems forever a most significant figure and model for identification in the life of his child' (Simos 1973). It is a poignant blow to see an admired and loved parent become an unpleasant or pathetic stranger.

The situation can be equally taxing to the married partner, although women are better prepared than their husbands for the role of housewife, nurse, and companion. If the man is left to care for his wife, he may find the sheer weight of household tasks overwhelming. Some men resent having to undertake jobs which they have been brought up to think of as 'women's work'; others strive, with varying degrees of success, to maintain their wife's previous standards of housework. In addition, at a stage of life when their own health and strength is declining, they have to find the inner resource to support a failing partner. They may rise courageously to the situation, sustained by years of happy marriage (see Mr Parry, Appendix 8, p.198). But if the marriage was less happy or if their own health is poor, the home situation can deteriorate alarmingly. The evidence is that married people will endure much hardship to avoid their partner being admitted to hospital (Grad and Sainsbury 1966). Such self-sacrifice puts special responsibility on the community service to be responsive to their needs.

(3) ENVIRONMENTAL DEFECTS

Housing
A less frequent cause of strain among relatives arises from defects in their environment. A sizeable minority find stairs a problem but one that can be overcome, if there is sufficient house space, by bringing the bed downstairs and installing a commode (Sanford 1975). Where relatives are old or handicapped themselves and living in poorly designed property, the local authority may be willing to make structural or other alterations to ease their chores (see Appendix 1, p.162).

Income
Shortage of money can prove another disincentive to home-care of the mentally infirm. A substantial proportion of relatives suffer a fall in their family income, especially if a wife or daughter has to give up a full-time job in order to care for the patient (Sainsbury and Grad 1966). In some instances, they are unaware that they are entitled to an attendance allowance. Timely help and advice with money problems may do more than take pressures off the family budget. It may, particularly if the local authority is willing to pay relatives for the care of their elderly dependent relative, relieve a weary middle-aged woman from the strain of trying to do two incompatible jobs.

Family stress
Some families are not only hard-up but divided in their loyalties.

141

Relatives' social life can be restricted by their additional responsibilities. Deprivation varies from the minor one of having to snatch
half-an-hour to do the shopping to the major inconvenience of
having had no time over a period of years for either an evening out
or a holiday (see Isaacs 1971; Isaacs, Livingstone, and Neville
1972). Difficulties multiply if it is a three-generation household.
Various surveys have shown that adverse effects on family life are
more likely where there are children (see Sainsbury and Grad
1966). In some instances their presence in the family may be sufficient to make an otherwise containable situation impossible
(Whelan and Bree 1954). Even if concern for the children does not
lead to the mother of a family withdrawing her support, she is aware
of being in a 'Catch-22' situation. Her loyalty to her sick parent is
in direct conflict with her concern for the happiness of other members of her family (see Appendix 8, p.196). A partial solution may
be day care, holiday relief, or intermittent admission to an in-
stitution ('floating-bed' arrangements). Such practical support
needs to be supplemented by more sustained counselling designed
to help the daughter to handle her patient skilfully and to help the
family to come to terms with the critical situation.

Help for the carers

MEDICAL AND ANCILLARY SUPPORT

A skilled medical diagnosis is at the root of proper care for the
mentally disturbed. Relatives need to know if the condition from
which the old person suffers is temporary and likely to improve or
whether it is permanent and likely to get worse. A few reject their
elderly dependants because they cannot face shouldering such a
burden for an indefinite period. They may be reassured if they
know that treatment can be given which will control pain, reduce
distressing symptoms or, at best, restore the invalid to an improved
state of health. Families should be told whether the treatment (by
drugs, dietary needs, or other methods) can be given at home or
whether the old person will need out-patient or in-patient care.
They should be told of the various support services and aids which
can be mobilized to make their task bearable. One family who six
years previously had given a home to the son's elderly father discovered by chance that he could have attended a nearby day centre.
Their view was that if they had been told of the service earlier
not only would their burden have been reduced, but more signifi-

cantly, the old man's deterioration might have been arrested. (See Mr Coates, Appendix 8, p.198).

SHORT-TERM HOSPITAL ADMISSION
Occasionally a mentally infirm old person is taken unexpectedly into hospital, or she may be admitted for observation, assessment, or in order to give the family time to recoup its strength. Such a break needs to be handled tactfully. Relatives do not always realize how greatly their interest can affect the health of the invalid. They may feel exhausted and tempted to stay at home, confident that their elderly dependant is being well cared for. They may not recognize how vital it is that they should continue to visit and to be concerned about the patient's welfare. In some areas it is possible for them to join hospital-based groups in which they can gain reassurance from discussing common problems with others facing a similar situation.

Occasionally this period of relief becomes a time when odious comparisons are made. 'It wasn't until I stopped,' admitted one daughter, 'that I realized how terribly tired I was. I should have been welcoming Dad back but I dreaded the return to upset nights and the endless washing. I kept praying the hospital would keep him in just one more day.' Another daughter in a similar position but with a family and a demanding job was told, 'Your mother will be ready to come home tomorrow'. She had to struggle with innumerable chores and a lot of antagonism from her family before reaching the hospital. She was a little late. The ward nurse said accusingly, 'Your mother has been waiting for ages, poor soul.' 'I can't tell you what I felt like saying to her,' said the daughter. 'The pity of it was, I was too exhausted and bad tempered to make a success of reuniting mother and the kids – if only they had given me a bit more warning, I might have done better.'

TIMELY DISCHARGE
Ward staff and social workers should keep relatives informed about the patient's progress and possibility of discharge. One old lady, who had been told that her husband was dying, disposed of his clothes only to be told that he was going to be sent home. She had to buy him a complete new outfit out of her small income. Much can be done to help relatives by returning the patient home at a helpful time and without undue haste. Weekend discharges may be particularly suitable where women, in full- or part-time employ-

ment, are nursing the invalid at home (see BASW 1977). In other circumstances weekend discharges should be avoided because support services are not available. Relatives like to be prepared for resuming their caring role and may welcome support at this time. On the other hand, they may resent being precipitated into a resumption of responsibilities without recourse to advice or practical help. This can only be to the disadvantage of the invalid.

NURSING HOME PLACEMENTS
The situation can be particularly challenging if family commitments, poor health, and distance from a failing parent make it impossible to give proper support. One daughter, with a lively teenage family and a husband who refused to accept his mother-in-law in his home, described her agony of mind when she tried to discover a suitable nursing home for her mother. It needed to be both accessible for visiting and acceptable as a long-term solution. She realized that finding such a place was a skilled job which might take a long time. She visited many nursing homes, depressed by the atmosphere and the number of women living together without privacy in one room. The cost of such accommodation and the prospects were equally unalluring. She longed to share her problem with a knowledgeable worker who would help her to take the painful decision.

LONG-TERM ADMISSION TO HOSPITAL
OR RESIDENTIAL CARE
Social workers and hospital staff can combine to make admission to either a home or a hospital – a process in which mutual respect and understanding can grow. The family needs to be encouraged to visit and to continue to give small services to the elderly patient. This is equally true for those who show reluctance to separate as for those who appear angrily to reject the invalid. (Compare Mr and Mrs Redding with Mr and Mrs Coates, Appendix 8, pp.196–8.) The anger, like the sadness, often cloaks feelings of guilt. Relatives, however long they have struggled to help, tend to feel they have failed if they cannot support the patient until she dies. They recover a sense of their own value if they can be made welcome and given jobs to do when the old person is in institutional care. Their loving attention will help to sustain her if ultimately she is able to return home or even if she is terminally ill.

FACING BEREAVEMENT

Occasionally one married partner or a single adult child has to face the herculean task not only of caring for a mentally infirm person, but also of coming to terms with her death and with the resulting practical problems of living alone. For men, who have rarely helped in the home, failure to manage household chores adds to their feeling of loss and inadequacy. Some can rise to the situation but others begin to neglect themselves if they are not given practical help and moral support.

Though loss of housewifely services may bear hard on some working-class men whose wives protected them from simple chores, it is women, and particularly middle-class women, who may find themselves unable to deal with forms and other practical jobs which their husbands used to do on their behalf. Their disadvantages are multiplied if their husband's papers have been neglected as a result of his infirmity. The challenge of managing on their own is as threatening to an elderly widow or widower as to a younger person with dependent children. This is particularly true when their moral and physical strength has been undermined by nursing a mentally infirm relative. Social workers may achieve a great deal by helping them to tackle some of these tasks. (See notes on legal matters, Appendix 2, pp.169–70.)

'Grief work'

Even when the short-term reaction to death is relief tinged with guilt, the long-term prospect may be bleak. Few have done their 'grief work' before their invalid dies. Mrs Webb was an exception. She had nursed her demented husband for six months before his death. When he died she told her adult children, 'I shall not grieve now. I did my grieving six months ago when the man I had loved for thirty-five years disappeared. I have just seen the body at last catching up with the spirit that left it then. I have looked after the body for all these months, not out of love but out of duty.' More often the deceased person is idealized or mourned as a lost child (Bree 1960). The process of working through bereavement is particularly taxing for those who have exhausted themselves trying to support a deteriorating personality. It is even worse if their own feelings for the once-loved person have become equivocal or even hostile. They may need skilled help in coming to terms with their loss.

COMPLEXITY OF TASK

Several brief case histories have been included in Appendix 8, pp.196–8). They are intended to show the range of situations in which relatives, caring for a mentally infirm old person, may need skilled help. Perhaps this is sufficient to demonstrate the complexity of the task. If not, there is independent evidence in a report designed to assess the reactions of the relatives of mentally ill people to attempts to offer social work help (Creer and Wing 1974). It cites examples of social workers who prove difficult, sometimes impossible to contact; give sympathy but fail to follow up with practical help; and ones who have no insight into the fears and anxieties which relatives endured. It concludes that the social services have failed in the past to appreciate 'the magnitude and complexity' of the problems faced by relatives who need all possible support to cope with what one of them described as 'the discordance of living constantly with abnormality'.

Summary

The overwhelming majority of mentally infirm elderly people are cared for by close relatives and others in the community. These people have to face problems which arise, first, because of the difficult behaviour of their elderly relatives; second, due to incapacities of their own or to a breakdown in their own health; third, because of defects in the environment including shortage of money and adverse effects on family life. The social services in collaboration with hospital and health staff need to develop a range of flexible support services designed to help relatives and other carers to continue to look after mentally disturbed elderly people in the community.

12 A BETTER FUTURE?

The extent of the problem

All forms of mental infirmity in the elderly, and especially those associated with brain failure, increase in frequency with the increasing age of the subject. In the next twenty years the most vulnerable groups, those aged 75 and over and especially those aged 85 and over, will increase in numbers. There will be no comparable growth in the population one generation younger, from which the major support of the aged is recruited. Nor will there be an increase in the number of young dependants who will be entering their first jobs and from whom the future health and social work staff have to be recruited. A situation which is already occasioning grave difficulty will almost certainly deteriorate in the next two decades. There is therefore a need for a planned strategy to deploy scarce resources to the best advantage of both ageing people and of those who care for them.

Reducing the incidence of mental illness

Research into the basic mechanisms of brain failure is going forward but not on a scale commensurate with the gravity of the problem. The work is complex and difficult. It requires very special resources. A great deal of research is being conducted on atherosclerosis, the underlying defect in vascular brain failure. Attention has been concentrated on discovering methods of preventing heart failure rather than of brain failure; these efforts have been rewarded by a slight drop in the incidence of myocardial infarction and stroke in certain parts of North America. No such changes have yet appeared in the UK and there are no figures about the prevalence of vascular brain failure, which is more difficult to define with precision. Certain measures can reduce the incidence and severity of vascular disease in general though not specifically of vascular disease of the brain. These include the prevention of high blood pressure, the control of diabetes, the avoidance of obesity and of excessive cigarette smoking, the avoidance of excessive animal fat in the diet, and the taking of adequate physical exercise. The general public has yet to demonstrate its willingness to accept and to act on these conclusions. In the future vascular brain failure may be prevented by better control of blood pressure; on the other hand improved treatment of myocardial infarction and other manifestations of heart disease in middle-aged patients may lead to the survival of more people who are at risk of developing vascular brain failure.

Several major lines of research are being pursued into the large-scale prevention of non-vascular brain failure. The possibility is being examined that this condition, or group of conditions, might be related to immunological abnormality, to the action of a slow virus or to the effect of aluminium. The first manifestations of the disease often occur in the sixth or seventh decades, so that preventive intervention will have to begin early. In this disease abnormalities have been discovered in the bio-chemistry of brain proteins and brain enzymes which leads to hopes that some chemical substance administered by mouth may be capable of replacing the missing enzymes and thus improving brain function.

The other causes of brain failure are numerous and offer some hope of prevention. However, it is inevitable that an increasing number of elderly surviving into very late life will suffer in many organs of the body from multiple pathological changes, almost any of which could be associated with diminishing brain function. Cancer in particular often manifests itself in this way.

Evidence in general suggests that there will be no substantial reduction in the proportion of the elderly population who carry the pathological changes associated with brain failure in the immediate future.

Medical management

If no breakthrough in medical treatment of susceptible patients is likely, a great drive will be necessary to control the established disease by improved medical care. The manifestations of the conditions of brain failure can be controlled even if the underlying causes cannot be removed. Drugs which aggravate the symptoms can be avoided and those which diminish and control its manifestations can be used more effectively. The medical profession is becoming increasingly aware that the terms 'senility' and 'dementia' need a more precise diagnosis which should be related to the history and symptoms of the individual patient. Drug research and development is concentrating on the compounds which can improve the metabolisms of surviving brain cells and on drugs which to some extent control inappropriate behaviour. It is increasingly recognized that people suffering from depression may appear to have brain failure, illustrating that accurate diagnosis is essential as a basis for effective treatment. Many drugs administered to old people for the management of insomnia, high blood pressure, and other diseases can have a deleterious effect on their brain function. More accurate prescribing might reduce brain disease from these causes. If screening procedures can be used more widely by GPs, this too could lead to earlier recognition of cases of brain failure and consequent earlier treatment of the disease.

Doctors cannot prevent or cure the major causes of brain failure, nor are they likely to be able to do so before the end of this century, but they can make a great contribution to the reduction of the problem by further improvements in their diagnosis and management of their elderly patients.

This could also lead to a control of distressing symptoms and be the basis of preserving the patients' independence. It could also give relatives understanding of how they could support effective medical treatment or be forearmed against a progressive deterioration in their elderly parent's condition. Social workers could be in a better position to marshal appropriate aids and services and to offer, as counsellors, informed support to hard-pressed relatives.

Resources

A great deal of the resources of the National Health Service and Social Services in the United Kingdom are already used in the management of the elderly mentally infirm. A recent estimate suggests that 35 per cent of health and personal social services expenditure is used on the treatment and care of those aged 65 and over and 20 per cent on those aged 75 and over (Owen 1976). This group occupies large numbers of beds in psychiatric and geriatric hospitals and in residential homes for the elderly. Geriatric beds comprise approximately 14 per cent of all hospital beds, but almost half the hospital in-patient population is aged 65 and over (Age Concern Research Unit 1977a). Those maintained in their own home often consume large resources from the domiciliary services and could consume more. The anticipated increase in old people, and particularly old people with mental infirmity, means that the health and social services will be subjected to greater pressure. In a society whose population of working age is proportionately decreasing, it hardly seems realistic to expect resources to keep pace with the pressure upon them. Resources include not only aids and services but the few trained staff.

Work in this area is not and cannot hope to be a highly attractive form of employment. Furthermore it must compete with other work such as care of the young mentally handicapped and of older people with severe disability. In these two areas technical advances in medical care have led to an increased rate of survival. An additional difficulty stems from the needs of elderly mentally infirm people for twenty-four hour observation. In the present economic climate residential staff and community workers are less willing to work at 'unsocial hours'. This makes for further difficulties in providing services and in recruiting staff. It may be that an inspired and disciplined use of voluntary workers may reduce but not remove this problem. Past evidence has suggested that where increased resources are allocated to expand services for the elderly with mental infirmity they are not necessarily used for the purpose. There is a need for public pressure or for pressure from special groups for the provision of adequate services for this under-privileged group.

Even if economic circumstances become more favourable, expansion of resources to meet expanding need is unlikely and possibly unacceptable. The aim of this chapter is to suggest means of preventing deterioration or even of creating useful improvements in treatment and support.

Environment, deprivation, and support

The social and demographic problems of old people have been outlined in Chapter 7. Many more people are surviving into extreme old age; 30 per cent live alone, of whom 80 per cent are women and 35 per cent are women aged 75 and over (Hunt 1978). Only a tiny minority of both sexes are cared for in institutions (6 per cent) compared with 30 per cent who live either with a relative or friend after the death of their partner. The majority live in their own homes.

The deprivation of those who live in residential homes is more likely to be of the spirit than of shortcomings in the physical environment (see pp.97–8). The deprivation of those living in their own homes is more likely to centre on poor housing conditions with relatively poor amenities and household goods. A minority have a meagre income and most have to spend a large share of it on the three basic necessities of food, fuel, and housing. They may also suffer from loneliness. These disadvantages increase with age as do physical and mental disabilities. The deprivations of old people living with their families include a decline in independence and anxiety about becoming a burden.

The kind of help needed varies with the circumstances and state of the individual. It ranges from the purely practical in the form of better pensions, sheltered housing, and adaptations to old property, to counselling support designed to give help to lonely, bereaved, or ill people. It extends to the family and friends who are caring for the frail elderly and thereby reducing the burden on the social and health services. They, too, may need practical help including payment, help with laundry or night-sitting as well as opportunities to talk about their difficulties and the feelings of guilt, anger, and despair with which they have to contend.

All this involves the use of a range of workers. Some of these, such as home helps, may have relatively narrow but nonetheless invaluable skills; others, like specialist social workers, need to have the ability to co-ordinate various services and the capacity to help old people to face decline and death while paradoxically seeking to improve their quality of life.

The structure of services
In the early 1970s the Health and Social Services of Great Britain each underwent a major reorganization. This proved costly and complex; some problems were solved but others have emerged as a consequence of the changes. It seems unlikely, and in some ways undesirable, that the present system should be altered for some time to come, although there are proposals to remove the area health authority tier from the existing structure. The problem is that the upheaval involved would distract efforts from providing services, to solving administrative and organizational problems. At present there is a structural separation between the two major

organizations responsible for the care of the mentally infirm. In addition both the National Health Service and the Social Service Departments have responsibilities for other groups in need so that their resources have to be rationed. The two services are financed in entirely different ways and their local boundaries do not coincide. Various suggestions have been made to improve co-operation between them. One is that provisions such as residential and day-care should be jointly financed so as to eliminate disputes about which service is responsible for the care of a particular old person. Another proposal is that the National Health Service should take over provision of residential care of the mentally infirm leaving the Social Service Departments to provide social work support from its field staff. It has also been suggested that the two services should have coterminous boundaries at district level. The National Association for Mental Health has suggested that where joint planning occurs, the hospital and local authority services for each district should agree not only to an initial programme but also to review progress at regular intervals (Mind 1973).

Even if the organization structures could be made more stream-lined collaboration would still be necessary. Individual members of families still cross boundaries and require medical or social work assistance when they are out of their catchment area. An exchange for short periods of workers from the two services could help to generate understanding of each other's roles and responsibilities. Health staff from assessment or geriatric units could work in residential institutions and care staff from old peoples' homes could give support in the geriatric hospital service. Radical reorganization seems unlikely at present and is no substitute for collaboration between the various disciplines.

Local collaboration
The form that co-operation takes depends in part on the structure of the local services. Collaboration is needed in the following areas.

(i) EARLY RECOGNITION OF ILLNESS
Effective ascertainment is the basis for early treatment of mental illness in the elderly. As old people are notoriously poor self-reporters, their needs have to be recognized by others (Williamson *et al.* 1964). One very effective way of doing this involves the primary health care team using its age and sex registers as a basis for regular medical screening of old people. The team, comprising doctors,

community nurse, health visitors, and other ancillary support, have the advantage of preserving 'the personal touch, so important to an elderly patient' (Stokoe 1965). The team would be strengthened by the addition of a social worker seconded from either the district Social Service Department or from a hospital (p.92).

Supplementary or alternative methods of ascertainment include the use of registers of old people compiled by district Social Service Departments. Where registers are available social workers can use them to screen elderly people most likely to be at risk and so enable them to be visited at regular intervals. In certain areas of the country this method is used, but it is costly to set up and to implement (p.90).

Another precautionary measure is to encourage those in close contact with elderly people living in their own homes to report to a central telephone number in the district Social Service Department any signs of deteriorating health. The telephonist would be responsible for alerting a named or key social worker (p.155). This worker would then arrange direct help or keep the old person's name on a waiting list subject to review.

A fourth method is to set up an inter-disciplinary early warning team on the lookout for deterioration in an elderly person's mental state. Candidates for this role would be the health visitor or the community nurse in the health services, and the home help or the voluntary visitor in the social services. Such workers would report first to their supervisor or to the organizer, who would alert the local GP and the named social worker.

The need for proper ascertainment procedures is illustrated by the alarmingly high percentage (87 per cent) of a sample of old people in an Edinburgh area who were found to be suffering from dementia without the knowledge of their own GP (Stokoe 1965).

(ii) ASSESSMENT

In the same way prompt and detailed assessment of a mentally infirm old person depends on collaboration between different disciplines. Assessment is concerned with the mental and physical health of an old person, and the way in which this is affected by her social circumstances. Assessment should be a team exercise in which the geriatrician, and/or a psychiatrist, in consultation with the old person's doctor, makes a diagnosis or prognosis of the patient's illness. They consult with ancillary health workers, social workers, and others, such as the home help organizer, so that the joint treatment plan can take account of both the home situation and history of the old person and of the availability of health and social service resources. The aim is to avoid initial misplacement which might well both delay recovery and impede rehabilitation. The team would aim to devise a treatment plan to suit the medical and social needs of the individual old person. It would depend on collaboration between the health and social services and on mutual understanding of each other's roles.

An assessment form and guidance notes to social workers have been included in Chapter 10 and in Appendix 4(b), pp.175–82. The aim is to give workers a framework within which they could exercise their skills. This is not a substitute for listening closely to old peoples' accounts of their situation or of discovering their view of their problems. The job of the professional is to strike a balance between accurate recording of 'the facts' of a situation and establishing personal empathy with the old person by recognizing her anxiety about the nature of the intervention which is planned (Gray 1978).

Team work of this kind can emerge from different structures. At present geriatric assessments units, which may overlap with psychiatric ones, are frequently used for diagnosis. They provide treatment facilities including out-patient or day-centre provision. Such units do not normally include a psychiatrist on their staff, so that in certain instances the medical procedure may be unnecessarily prolonged. They may also be prevented from functioning properly because patients who need hospital care but not specialist treatment cannot be transferred if there is no vacant bed. Another drawback arises when, although an old person is suitable for sheltered housing, there is no placement available, or when the tenancy of her own home has been allowed to lapse. Further, there is a danger that once a hospital bed is found, it is regarded as a solution to the problem. With resources in short supply professional workers may, without regard to the old person's wishes, collude with exhausted relatives by allowing the situation to persist.

There are no simple solutions to these problems. However, if more psychogeriatric units were created this would reduce the time involved on the medical assessment procedure. The misuse of specialist unit beds could be reduced if a standing committee were set up to discuss and to work out a sensible system of allocating beds. Representatives from general hospitals and from geriatric units should be on such a committee. In addition the assessment unit team could co-opt a representative from the housing department who would keep an eye on the special needs of the elderly mentally infirm for available sheltered housing. The unit could also call regular case conferences in which a shared decision could be made on an appropriate treatment plan. At these meetings progress on past cases would be reviewed at specified intervals. A matter of special concern would be whether the patient could be returned to her own home or to another housing unit in the community. Such meetings would require a clear agenda, and should be brief and businesslike. On rare occasions they could be supplemented with social meetings in which all members of the unit team could get to know each other better and could learn about each other's professional skills.

(iii) A NAMED OR KEY SOCIAL WORKER

A vital member of the assessment team would be a social worker with special knowledge of the personality and background of the old person concerned. This worker could be drawn from a hospital, from a primary health care team (see p.92), or from the area office based on the neighbourhood in which the patient lives. She should be designated or 'named' and her responsibilities should be similar to those of the first professional person involved in a non-accidental injury case. She should marshal appropriate services to give support to the old person or her relatives in a home situation. She should review progress (at six-monthly intervals as for children in care) and ensure that the treatment plan is carried out with due regard to the wishes of the old person. She should act as a link between the medical and social services. Such workers should be identifiable, accountable, and responsible to both the inter-disciplinary team and to the old person and her family. The primary client should be the old person.

(iv) APPROPRIATE CARE IN
AN INSTITUTIONAL SETTING

Where either short-term or long-term hospital admission is necessary, the named social worker should have responsibility, in collaboration with medical colleagues, to ease the process of admission and discharge for both the old person and her carers (pp.143–4). She would have to make sure that no precipitous action, such as selling up a home or disposing of furniture, would jeopardize the patient's return home.

In certain instances she might be instrumental in arranging for short periods of convalescence in a residential home or for intermittent admission to a hospital in order to relieve relatives. In such circumstances residential institutions would appear to have two roles. The first would be to offer short-term care, a refuge or a place for rest and recuperation before the old person returns home. The second would be to give primarily physical care to those too fragile and infirm to remain on their own in the community. Social casualties should be given domiciliary support, special housing, or fostering care, and should not end up in this kind of residential accommodation.

Pressure on hospital beds might be eased if residential homes fulfilled this rather narrower role, which is already beginning to be forced on them by the process of ageing and failing health among existing residents. Homes should allocate a high percentage of their beds to hospitals; a certain number, depending on local need, being available to the mentally infirm elderly. They should do so on the understanding that the person concerned would be admitted or re-admitted to the unit or ward when appropriate. Interchange should be on the basis of the old person's needs and not on an exchange system (Blair, Constable, and Davies 1975).

The result of such a policy might be to relieve some pressure on long-stay hospital care. In a situation of staff shortage it is these patients who suffer most. They need adequate treatment, rehabilitation, and diversional programmes with the staff to run them. One possible way of dealing with an acute shortage of medical and para-medical staff would be to appoint qualified voluntary organizers who could complement full-time specialized services and provide a link with the outside world for many patients (Mind 1973). In a similar way support in the new-style residential homes could be drawn from named social workers and other Social Service Department staff working in collaboration with voluntary workers. The aims would again be to improve the quality of life of residents and to preserve their ties with relatives and friends in their old neighbourhood.

Collaboration costs little and can achieve much. It requires initiative, elasticity, and personal contact; it tests workers from different disciplines, requiring them to empathize with colleagues as well as with patients or clients. It is perhaps the best hope for better services in later life.

Specialization and training

(i) MEDICAL STAFF

In 1975, according to the DHSS statistics for England and Wales, of 28,922 total medical staff, only 3·5 per cent work in geriatrics, 2·7 per cent as consultants (Age Concern Research Unit 1977a). The approved ratio (British Geriatrics Society medical staff norm) is two consultants for every 250 beds; in fact there is only one consultant for every 210 beds, a shortfall of 68 per cent. This illustrates the abundant need for encouraging specialization in the field of geriatrics.

The hope for the future is that more medical students will be encouraged to take up the geriatric option. Specialist training courses should also be offered to doctors who have qualified for some years in order to update their knowledge of geriatrics. This training should be useful to GPs, either to allow one partner in a group practice to concentrate on elderly patients, or to allow him to acquire a part-time hospital attachment. There would still be the same need for support and advice from consultants in cases of exceptional difficulty. It would give scope for an expansion in the appointment of geriatricians and psychiatrists as consultants with special responsibility for the care of the mentally infirm (Mind 1973).

(ii) FIELD WORKERS IN
SOCIAL SERVICE DEPARTMENTS

A study conducted between 1974 and 1977, sponsored by the DHSS, set out to discover the way in which field social workers approach and organize their work and their feelings about it. The study, *Social Service Teams: The Practitioners' View* (DHSS 1978), covered workers in various local authorities including urban and rural settings in the United Kingdom. The general view was that the elderly were a low priority for social workers compared with work in families where children were at risk or delinquent. This did not necessarily mean that less money or time was spent on older people but rather that it was not the best qualified and experienced social workers who generally visited the elderly. Without devaluing present contributions, efforts should be made to redress this imbalance and to ensure that old people get a fair share of skilled workers' time.

One way of doing this would be to encourage special training both at basic diploma and advanced level to produce specialists who could be both a source of excellence in practice and the means of offering supervision to less experienced social workers. The British Association of Social Workers has offered a short document outlining *Guidelines for Social Work with the Elderly* (BASW 1977). The Central Council for Education and Training has issued *Guidelines for Post-Qualifying Studies*. The aim should be to use these documents as the basis for providing appropriate training on degree courses and professional diploma courses and as an impetus to offering short-training modules to those without specialist instruction in this field.

Courses should also be devised to help career grade social workers who would like to undertake work with the elderly. The British Association of Social Workers has presented a report on how the career grade can be implemented (Andrews 1975). The aim should be to reach a higher general level of competence within an area team with possibly one social worker undertaking this specialism and with a suitably qualified career grade officer available to give guidance and supervision.

(iii) VOLUNTARY WORKERS

This group has pioneered and continues to lead the way in aspects of work with the elderly (see Chapter 8). Their efforts should be fostered and Social Service Departments should develop new ways of co-operating with them. When specialist skills are in such short supply social workers will need to find a formula of co-operation which overcomes Trade Union fears that volunteers may be used as cheap labour. Joint training courses should be offered to deepen the understanding of the professional and the volunteer of the roles and the skills of the other.

(iv) RESIDENTIAL WORKERS

There is need for both in-service and post-experience training for these workers on courses designed to increase their understanding of and ability to relate to the mentally infirm. They should be offered practice placements with hospital staff and on area teams as well as joint courses with health and social work staff.

Supervision

Inexperienced and untrained social workers, welfare assistants, and others without specialist training should have easy access to advice and supervision. Supervisors could include the named social worker, a member of the first-line management, or professionally trained social worker with a specialism in this field. Career grade social workers, who in future will be expected to undertake a rigorous training, would also be suitable to act both as supervisors and as consultants. Their time would be limited by their substantial caseload.

Experienced voluntary workers normally supervise new recruits within their service. When working in collaboration with the Social Service Department, volunteers may also welcome access to supervising officers. The ultimate responsibility for such oversight and for the standard of the service offered would then rest with the professionally trained social worker.

Residential workers are in even greater need of support on the job. They may get help from staff discussions and from an effective management team. Care staff also need reassurance and advice on a planned basis from experienced workers in their specialism. Ideally this should be given by trained colleagues with long-term experience, or by Officers in Charge or their Deputies (Blair, Constable, and Davies 1975).

Multi-disciplinary courses

Jointly shared training of medical and health staff with social workers at an undergraduate level, with an exchange of practical placements, should be the basis of increased mutual understanding and should promote collaboration.

Multi-disciplinary conferences would be another way of sharing knowledge and of creating a pressure group which could inform public opinion and direct the Government's attention to a growing section of the population in need of help.

Proper, effective, and sensitive help of elderly people depends on a multi-disciplinary approach. Workers from different disciplines need to understand each other's roles and to combine together for the benefit of each elderly person they are trying to support. They may even be able to support each other by sharing the strain involved in this kind of work. They should seek to be realistic and tenacious in their efforts. Nevertheless they should come to terms with the fact that in some instances (even most instances at the end of life) there is no practical solution to an individual's predicament. Their greatest service will be in helping an old person to find resignation and peace of mind.

159

Summary
The incidence of mental infirmity increases in later life. Grave pressures are put on the hospital and community services when the number surviving into late old age is also going up. This problem is not likely to be reduced by an immediate breakthrough in medical treatment. It has to be contained instead by better diagnosis, management, and use of community resources. Hospital and local authority staff will need to collaborate in drawing up joint plans and in reviewing them at intervals. There is an acute need for more resources and more personnel to help both the elderly infirm and their carers.

APPENDIX 1: LEGISLATION

The principal Acts affecting those working with the elderly mentally infirm are as follows:

National Health Service Act (1946);
National Assistance Act (1948);
Mental Health Act (1959);
Health Service and Public Health Act (1968);
Local Authority Social Services Act (1970);
Chronically Sick and Disabled Persons Act (1970).

Sections of these Acts, and other pieces of legislation relevant to the elderly mentally infirm, are summarized below.

The Local Government Act (1929)
Part 1 – Poor Law (Sections 1–20 inclusive).

Section 1   The functions of each poor law authority transferred to the council of the county or county borough comprising the poor law area.

Section 5   Assistance for special groups should be provided otherwise than by poor relief through powers conferred under earlier Acts, including: The Public Health Act (1875); The Government Act (1888); The Mental Health Deficiency Act (1913); The Maternity and Child Welfare Act (1918); The Blind Person's Act (1920); etc. 'Assistance' to include maintenance and treatment at hospitals and other places.

161

Section 6 Local Authority Public Assistance Committees to be set up to administer functions mentioned in Section 5.

Section 19 The functions of the board of guardians under the Poor Law Act (1927) to be transferred to the council of the county or county borough, including the duty to provide relief for the poor.

Promotion of domiciliary services for the elderly

National Assistance Act (1948) as amended (1962); a local authority *may* with the approval of the Minister to such an extent as he may direct, provide recreational facilities and meals to persons in their own homes.

Under Section 45(1) Health Services and Public Health Act (1968) a local authority *may* with the approval of the Minister of Health and to such extent as he *may* direct *shall*, make arrangements for promoting the welfare of old people. The use of this power can take many forms. DHSS circular (1971b) has indicated the following:

(i) to provide meals and recreation in the home and elsewhere;

(ii) to inform the elderly of services available to them and to identify elderly people in need of services;

(iii) to provide facilities or assistance in travelling to and from home for the purpose of participating in services provided by the authority or similar services;

(iv) to assist in finding suitable households for boarding elderly persons;

(v) to provide visiting and advisory services and social work support;

(vi) to provide practical assistance in the home, including assistance in the carrying out of works of adaptation or the provision of any additional facilities designed to secure greater safety, comfort, or convenience;

(vii) to contribute to the cost of employing a warden on welfare functions in warden-assisted housing schemes;

(viii) to provide warden services for private housing.

Under Section 45(2) a local authority may recover from persons availing themselves of any service provided ... under this section such charges (if any), as ... the authority may determine, whether generally or in the circumstances of any particular case.

Under Section 45(3) a local authority may employ as their agent for the purpose of this section any voluntary organization having for its sole principal object ... the promotion of the welfare of old people.

Under Section 13 Local Authority Social Services Departments have a duty to provide on such a scale as is adequate for the needs of their area ... home help* for households where such help is required owing to the presence of:

  (i) a person who is suffering from illness;
 (ii) lying in or expectant mother;
(iii) aged person;
 (iv) a person handicapped as a result of having suffered from illness or congenital deformity;
  (v) a child below the upper limit of compulsory school age.

In addition every authority shall have power to provide or arrange for the provision of laundry facilities for householders for which home help is being, or can be, provided under this section.

Again under *Section 13(2)* it is possible for a local authority to levy a charge for this service. Some authorities have extended this service in various ways, for example:

  (i) *family aides* who are sent to live in households for temporary period to act as mother substitutes to children whose mothers have to go to hospital, etc.;
 (ii) *good neighbours* (sometimes paid, sometimes not) who agree to undertake 'good neighbour' services for nearby elderly or handicapped people or who provide practical day care in other ways.

Funeral arrangements. Under Section 50 of the National Assistance Act (1948) the local authority are obliged to arrange a simple funeral for those unable to afford one. In such instances they claim the death grant. If this does not cover the whole cost of the funeral, the authority may recover the difference from the dead person's estate or from liable relatives. A local authority may also arrange for the funeral of an elderly person in residential or temporary accommodation. In certain circumstances, hospital authori

---

* Prior to 1 April 1971, the responsibility for the provision of the home help services rested with the local health authority, but on that date under the Local Authority Social Service Act (1970) the responsibility passed to the newly constituted Local Authority Social Services Departments.

ties have power to arrange and pay for the burial of patients who die in NHS hospitals where arrangements have not been made by their relatives.

Institutional Care

Under Section 21(1) National Assistance Act (1948) it shall be *the duty* of every local authority . . . to provide 'residential accommodation for persons who by reason of age, infirmity or other circumstances are in need of care and attention which is not otherwise available to them'.

Residential accommodation should be available regardless of a person's means.

Residential accommodation should not be provided for people whose need is only for provision of suitable housing.

A local authority cannot be required to provide accommodation for a person who needs hospital treatment. In 1957 the Ministry of Health issued two circulars 14 and 57, one to local authorities, one to hospitals, indicating the criteria to be used for determining their respective responsibilities.

The *local authorities* are responsible (apart from active elderly persons) for:

(i) Care of the otherwise active resident in a Welfare Home during minor illnesses which may well include a short period in bed.

(ii) Care of the infirm (including the senile) who may need help in dressing, toilet, etc., and may need to live on the ground floor because they cannot manage stairs, and may spend part of the day (or longer periods in bad weather) in bed.

(iii) Care of those elderly persons in a Welfare Home who have to take to bed and are not expected to live more than a few weeks (or exceptionally months) and who would, if in their own home, stay there because they could not benefit from treatment or nursing care beyond that which can be given at home, and whose removal to hospital away from their familiar surroundings and attendants would be felt to be inhumane.

(iv) Care of those elderly persons in a Welfare Home for whom any necessary nursing care would be given by relatives, etc., with the help or advice of the home nurse if they were living in their own home. In welfare homes this care should be given by attendants, assisted or advised by the visiting home nurse in the small welfare home, or by a small staff with nursing qualifications or experience in the larger homes.

Hospital Services

Apart from the acute sick and others needing active treatment, who are clearly the responsibility of the hospital authority, the latter's responsibility also extends to the following:

(i) Care of the chronic bedfast who may need little or no medical treatment but do require prolonged nursing care over months or years.

(ii) Convalescent care of the elderly sick who have completed active treatment but are not yet ready for discharge to their own homes or to welfare homes.

(iii) Care of the senile, confused, or disturbed patient who is, owing to his mental condition, unfit to live a normal community life in a welfare home.

It is not regarded as the responsibility of the hospital authority to give all medical or nursing care needed by an old person, however minor the illness or however short the stay in bed; nor to admit all those who need nursing care because they are entering the last stage of their lives.

Section 21(5) National Assistance Act (1948) states that residential accommodation shall include board and other services, amenities, and requisites. MOH circular (1957) indicates that a home for elderly people should be a substitute for a normal home and meet all reasonable requirements of the residents including clothing, extra comforts, recreational facilities, books, radio, TV, opportunities for religious worship, etc.

Section 26 enables a local authority to make arrangements with voluntary organizations for the provision of accommodation in lieu of or in supplementation of local authority provision. This power has been extended by Section 44 Health Services and Public Health Act (1968).

Under Section 37 it is an offence to carry on a disabled persons' or old persons' home without being registered by the local authority. The local authority must keep a register of such homes and can refuse registration if the staffing, premises, or management of the home are not satisfactory. There are regulations governing the inspection of such homes and the DHSS may make regulations for the guidance of local authorities concerning the number of people

165

who may be accommodated in a particular home, the facilities and services to be provided, etc.

Under Section 48 Movable property of anyone who is admitted to a hospital or a home (residential accommodation), or a similar place, must be looked after if no suitable arrangements can otherwise be made. Reasonable expenses can be reclaimed by the authority.

Under Section 44 of the Health Services and Public Health Act (1968) the power granted local authorities to provide accommodation themselves was extended to providing accommodation by voluntary organizations or other registered providers.

Under Section 6 of the Mental Health Act (1959) the local authority may provide residential accommodation as well as ancillary or supplementary services for persons who are or have been suffering from mental disorder.

Compulsory removal of persons needing care and attention

Section 47 National Assistance Act (1948) as amended by National Assistance (Amendment) Act (1951) gives certain powers to Medical Officers of Health (Community Physicians) to arrange for the removal of persons needing care and attention who (a) are suffering from grave chronic disease or being aged, infirm, or physically incapacitated are living in insanitary conditions and are (b) unable to devote to themselves, and are not receiving from other persons, proper care and attention.

It is necessary for the MOH (Community Physician) to certify in writing that he is satisfied after thorough enquiry and consideration that in the interests of any such person or for preventing injury to the health of, or serious nuisance to, other persons it is necessary to remove such a person from the premises in which he is residing. Application can then be made by the appropriate authority, or MOH (Community Physician) if so authorized, to a court of summary jurisdiction for an order. The court may, if satisfied, order the removal of the person to a suitable hospital or other place and his detention there. The period covered by the order may not be more than three months at any one time. The person concerned or the person in charge of him must be given seven days notice of the intended application. No order can be made unless the manager of the premises to which the removal is to be made has been heard in the proceedings or has received seven days' notice of the intended application.

In the case of an emergency, under the provision of the National Assistance (Amendment) Act (1951), where the MOH (Community Physician) and other Medical Practitioner certify that it is necessary in his own interests for a person to be removed without delay from the premises where he is residing, an application for a removal order can be made to the appropriate Magistrates' Court (or single Justice) without giving the usual seven days' notice. An order made under these circumstances can be made for not more than three weeks. If an extension is needed, normal procedure must be followed.

Application for revocation by or on behalf of the person in respect of whom the order was made cannot be applied for until six weeks after the order was first made. The application should be submitted to the magistrates' court which first made the order.

The Mental Health Act (1959)

Where psychiatric treatment is required on an in-patient basis the majority of patients voluntarily enter hospital. Where it is necessary to override the patient's wishes in the interest of society, the above Act lays down the procedure for compulsory admission to hospital. In the context of the Act 'mental disorder' means mental illness, arrested or incomplete development of mind, psychopathic disorder, or any other disorder or disability defined within Section 4.

Action may be taken under the following sections.

Section 25 When a patient is admitted to hospital and *detained there for observation* for a period not exceeding *28 days* if:

(i) she is suffering from a mental disorder of a nature or degree which warrants detention;
(ii) she ought to be detained in the interests of her own health and safety or with a view to the protection of other persons.

An application must be supported by the medical recommendation of two doctors, one of whom must be specially approved by the local authority for this type of work and one of whom should preferably have been acquainted with the patient. The application may be made either by the nearest relative of the patient or by a social worker in the Social Services Department.

167

Section 26 When a patient is admitted to hospital and *detained there for treatment* for up to a year if she is suffering from a mental disorder of a nature or degree which warrants detention for medical treatment, and she ought to be given treatment in the interests of her own health and safety or for the protection of other persons. An application giving reasons to be made on the written recommendation of two medical practitioners. If an early discharge is granted, the patient may be recalled without the need for a fresh application up to the end of the twelve month period.

Section 29 In cases of urgent necessity an *emergency application* can be made to admit a patient to hospital and to detain her there for *observation* for a period *not exceeding seventy-two hours*. In this instance the recommendation need be supported by only one medical practitioner.

Section 30 In the case of a patient who is already in hospital but not being detained there, if a medical practitioner in charge of her treatment concludes that the patient should be detained in hospital, he may apply for 'admission'. The doctor must submit his application to the hospital managers. In such instances the patient can be detained in hospital *for treatment for three days* beginning with the day on which the doctor's report is received.

For further discussion of this Act see DHSS (1978a) in which the Government makes proposals for changes in powers available under the sections listed above, and DHSS (1975).

APPENDIX 2:
BRIEF LEGAL NOTES

Power of attorney

When an old person's health is declining she may give power of attorney to another person. This is a document which grants a person or persons the power to act on another's behalf. The power may be limited to one named transaction applying for example, to the sale of the old person's house, or it may be an unfettered authority applying to all the old person's affairs. There is a statutory form which should be completed when wide powers of attorney are given, and specially drafted forms for limited transactions. A solicitor normally deals with the documents. He must be satisfied, if necessary on medical advice, that the old person concerned is capable of giving her consent.

Court of Protection

If the solicitor is of the view that the old person is not capable of granting power of attorney to another person because of inability to think rationally, he will advise application to the Court of Protection under Part VIII of the Mental Health Act (1959) for a receivership or other management order. The advantage is that the old person's affairs will be managed by a professional person who will be unable to sell her assets without the prior consent of the Court of Protection. The intervention of the Court of Protection is to be recommended when a number of relatives have interest in the old person's affairs or where the assets are considerable. The process, however, is reputed to be long drawn out and costly. Applications may be made to the Court of Protection directly, either by a relative, or a social worker, or a solicitor to: 25 Store Street, London EC1E 7PB (01 636 6877).

Making a will

It is always helpful if an old person is advised to make a will. It is generally better that such a will be prepared by a solicitor. If the old person thinks that she cannot afford legal services, she should apply for legal advice and assistance which is available for those whose weekly income is low, and who have small savings. The solicitor's help in such instances will either be free or for a small charge only, normally between £15 and £20. The full cost will be made clear before the will is drawn up.

A solicitor must be satisfied, where an old person's mental health is in decline, that if she wishes to make a will she has full testamentary capacity: that is, that she is capable of making a will which expresses her own personal choice and preference and is freely undertaken. The solicitor may ask for medical advice on the old person's mental state and may sign the will himself and have it countersigned by a doctor. If the solicitor is not satisfied that the old person understands the nature of the document he is drawing up, he should refuse to make the will.

Proving a will

Relatives or others who benefit under a will should apply to the executor(s) of that will. Before any part of the estate of a dead person can be used or paid out, it is necessary to apply for a *grant of probate* which has to be obtained if the person who left a will named an executor to wind up the estate. It is a legal formality which grants him the right to deal with it.

Where no will exists

Where there is *no will* application should be made normally to the next of kin. In such instances the Probate Registry will have to grant *letters of administration* which gives the right to a named person or persons to deal with a dead person's estate. The Probate Registry is at 'Astley House', 23 Quay St, Manchester M3 4AT (061 834 4319 or 4553). In all the above matters it is recommended that a solicitor should be consulted. For further information see:

Josling (1976). Persons mentally disordered are discussed on page 43, and the statutory form giving powers of attorney in Appendix 1, page 91;

The Powers of Attorney Act (1973) Cmnd. 4473, especially paragraphs 25 to 27;

Leaflet on will making from The Law Society (113 Chancery Lane, London WC2A 1PL);

Citizen's Advice Bureaux, who have lists of local solicitors' forms.

APPENDIX 3:
FINANCIAL CONCESSIONS

The following financial and other concessions are available to help elderly people and their relatives and carers.

Supplementary pensions
Such a pension, which is designed to bring a person's income up to a guaranteed weekly level, may be claimed by people who have reached statutory retirement age. Those who are dependent on a state pension with small personal savings, who are not in full-time work, are generally eligible for a supplementary pension.

The weekly requirements are made up of a sum for living expenses, an amount for rent, mortgage repayments and rates, and certain discretionary additions. The latter may include money for heating and special diets in appropriate cases, and, in exceptional circumstances, for such items as clothes, bedding, and furniture.

Fares for hospital visits may be claimed by people receiving a supplementary pension. In some instances relatives may be able to benefit from this help. People living in local authority old persons' homes may generally obtain a supplementary pension if their weekly income is not sufficient to meet the charges made by the home and to leave a margin for personal spending. Claims from people in private nursing homes are decided on an individual basis. Old people living with others may also claim supplementary pensions and will receive a small nominal amount for their contribution towards the rent. The Department of Health and Social Security administers the supplementary benefit scheme on behalf of the Supplementary Benefits Commission. (For details, ask for leaflet SB.1 at the Post Office.

Rate and rent rebates

Retirement pensioners on low incomes may be entitled to rent rebates unless they are already receiving a supplement to their pension which covers the rates. The amount of rebate depends on the income, size of household, and the rates payable.

Rent rebates are available to local authority tenants, and rent allowances to tenants of housing associations and private landlords. The amount paid depends on the same circumstances as apply to rate rebates (above). As in the case of rate rebates, those on supplementary benefit who receive an addition for rent are not eligible. Apply to the Director of Finance of your local council.

Transport and other concessions

Some local authorities make arrangements under which retirement pensioners can travel on local bus and rail services without charge or at a reduced fare. Eligibility and the nature of the concession are determined by the local authority. British Rail operates a scheme under which retirement pensioners travel at half fare if they purchase a yearly Senior Citizen Railcard.

Some local authorities reduce the fee for retirement pensioners attending further education courses. Licences for television sets in old people's homes and in housing schemes with communal facilities are available at a reduced rate. Some cinemas, theatres, launderettes, dry cleaners, hairdressers, and other firms lower their charges for old people.

Attendance allowance

Many elderly people, and the elderly mentally infirm are examples of these, are ill or disabled and need a lot of care. A tax-free attendance allowance is paid for people who need frequent attention or continual supervision by day and night. A lower rate is payable for those needing such attention by either day or night. These requirements have to be satisfied for six months before the allowance is paid. For more information, ask for Department of Health and Social Security leaflet N.1 205.

Invalid care allowance

A non-contributory, taxable invalid care allowance is payable to people who are unable to work because they are spending at least thirty-five hours a week in caring for a severely disabled relative who is receiving an attendance allowance. There are also additions for a wife and a dependent child or children. This allowance is not payable if the applicant is receiving the same amount or more from another social security benefit. Those receiving such an allowance are credited with national insurance contributions. In general, married women cannot qualify for the invalid care allowance. Explanatory leaflet N.1 212 with claim form D.S. 700 attached is available from local Social Security offices.

In addition to the above concessions, a *Mobility Allowance*, currently available to those aged between 5 and 60 will be extended to men aged 65 and over, and women aged 60 and over, by the end of 1979. See leaflet N.1 211.

For further information, consult your local Social Security office, the local Old People's Welfare Council, or your nearest Citizen's Advice Bureau, and see:

Age Concern (latest edition) *Your Rights For Pensioners;*
Central Office of Information (1977) *Care of the Elderly in Britain,* Pamphlet 121. London: HMSO;
Public Relations Unit, Metropolitan Borough of Stockport (1976) *Sixty Onwards; A Handbook for People of Retirement Age and Above;*
Disability Alliance (1978) *Disability Rights Handbook for 1978;*
DHSS (1978) *Which Benefit?* (F.B.2 Handbook);
DHSS (1978) *Social Security Benefit Rates* (N.1 196/November 1978).

APPENDIX 4: GUIDELINES
FOR SOCIAL WORKERS

4(a) Symptoms of mild and severe intrinsic brain failure and of extrinsic brain failure

1 *Lapses in personal hygiene:* refusal to bathe; refusal to wash; failure to close door while using toilet; failure to flush toilet; soilage of floor around toilet; failure to cleanse self after defecation; soilage of other parts of house; urination other than in toilet, not due to incontinence; defecation other than in toilet, not due to incontinence; offensive odour; concealment of soiled garments; faecal staining of hands; smearing of faeces on body; smearing of faeces on clothing, linen, furniture; expectoration.

2 *Lapses in feeding and dressing:* refusal of food; objectionable feeding habits; unusual untidiness in dress; inappropriate choice of dress; failure to fasten clothing; failure to close fly; putting on garments incorrectly; stripping off all clothing.

3 *Impairment of domestic skills:* failure to prepare meals; food allowed to go bad; kettle burned out; pots and pans burned out; gas turned on and not lit; inappropriate materials consumed; excessive fires maintained; accumulation of rubbish; insufficient food purchased; excessive food purchased; house unclean.

4 *Lack of judgement and prudence:* irresponsible expenditure of money; refusal to pay bills; failure to collect pension; irresponsible gifts; failure to observe proper precautions in traffic; formation of inappropriate associations.

5 *Cognitive errors:* failure to recognize close relatives, friends; denial or unawareness of location (in absence of recent change of location); getting lost in a familiar environment; 'going back' in time; repetitive questioning; 'following around'; repetitive utterances; going to bed by day fully dressed; refusal to go to bed at night; going into wrong bed; going into wrong room; denial of misbehaviour.

6 *Personality and interpersonal relations:* temper tantrums; groundless accusations; rejection of affection.

7 *Miscellaneous offensive behaviours:* verbal sexual advances; physical sexual advances; sexual exposure; restless wandering by day indoors; restless wandering by day outdoors; restless wandering at night indoors; restless wandering at night outdoors; knocking at neighbours' doors; shouting or banging indoors; shouting or banging outside neighbours' houses; pilfering.

4(b) Assessment of elderly client at risk in the community—Guidelines

1 Old people tend not to ask help for themselves. Their needs have to be recognized by others, including social workers.

2 An informed medical opinion (diagnosis/prognosis) should be one of the social worker's first aims if her help is to be effective.

3 If old people are living in private households, their local GP has ultimate responsibility for their physical and mental health.

4 Social workers and GPs should try to get to know each other personally and keep each other informed about the help they are giving to the old person.

5 The social worker, the geriatrician, and the psychiatrist will only want people to leave their homes for the shortest possible time while appropriate help is given.

6 Old people are more content and less confused in a familiar environment.

7 Free exchange of information between health and social work staff can only be to the advantage of the patient.

8 Only in an emergency situation should assessments be made on on the basis of one interview.

9 Social workers should try to get direct information *from* the old

person and should give information directly *to* the old person unless she is too ill to understand.

10 The main aim in an initial interview is to get information, but it may be possible to give reassurance and to establish crucial relationships at this time.

11 Questions should always be open-ended.

12 Social workers should give all parties a courteous hearing, noting inconsistencies and incongruities in their accounts of events.

13 They should be aware that even the most disturbed old lady may sometimes speak the truth, and even the most truthful relative may unintentionally mislead.

14 The social worker may have to recognize that all she can do is to help relatives and friends to tolerate difficult behaviour and be available to give reassurance and advice about the appropriate time to intervene.

15 Social workers should avoid suggesting a place in a Home unless there is no alternative.

16 Old people need careful preparation for either reception into a Home or Hospital and for discharge from them.

17 Old people must give their free consent to having their houses cleaned or their property destroyed.

18 Elderly people like anyone else should be allowed to take some risks.

19 Social workers should continue to keep in touch with elderly clients if they go into long-term institutional care.

20 Eccentricity, unhygienic habits, or nuisance behaviour are not sufficient grounds for removing old people from their homes.

21 In making a decision about removal consider whether the squalor pre-dated the decline in the old person's mental state.

22 Social workers should ask themselves if medical treatment and convalescence, combined with practical help, will enable the patient better to manage her own affairs?

23 The only grounds for compulsory admission should be that the old person, who is too disturbed to have insight, is endangering her own health or that of others, and unless she is restrained the result may be serious.

Assessment Form

I. COMPLAINT

Your department has been asked to see an elderly person who is behaving in an odd, unusual, disturbing, and/or bizarre fashion.

1 Name, address, and telephone number.
2 Age/Date of Birth
3 Referral   (a) by old person
             (b) by relative
             (c) by neighbour or friend
             (d) by social worker
             (e) doctor
             (f) anyone else.

4 Describe the nature of the complaint or request for help.
5 Is this elderly person known to you? If yes, consult your records.
   If no,   (a) consult the register of old people for your area if
                 applicable
          (b) consult colleagues
          (c) consult other relevant services.

II. HOME VISITS

1 What is the old person's situation and history? Discuss directly
   with elderly person wherever possible.
   (Describe appearance of old person, home, people in household,
   neighbourhood.)
2 Are any of the following circumstances present?

  (a) aged 80 or over
  (b) widowed
  (c) recently bereaved (specify)
  (d) recently moved home (how long has he/she lived at present
      address)
  (e) just discharged from geriatric hospital (give name of hospital)
  (f) lives alone
  (g) lives in a lodging house or as a lodger in a private household
  (h) socially isolated.

3 What is the old person feeling about the present situation? (On
   the basis of what he/she says or does describe state of mind,
   speech, facial expression, body movements, attitude to and
   awareness of her own illness.)
4 According to those who know her well is the behaviour complained of:

  (a) usual *for this old person*

    (b) more exaggerated than is usual

    (c) unusual for this old person.

5 Has the illness or situation arisen suddenly?
  (Give details including dates if possible.)
6 Has the situation or illness developed slowly?
  (Give details including dates if possible.)
7 Has the old person seen his/her GP lately?
  (Give date of latest visit, if possible.)
  Give name, address, telephone of old person's GP.
  How often does he call?
  What treatment is he giving?
  If GP has not visited, ask old person if he may do so.
  Ask if you may speak to the GP about the old person's health.
8 If available give brief details of GP's diagnosis/prognosis of old
   person's state of health.
  If not available, consult GP as a matter of urgency.
9 Is the old person receiving help from any of the following
   agencies or services?
  (Give names, addresses, and telephone numbers where possible.)

    (a) other social service worker
    (b) home help
    (c) health visitor
    (d) community nurse
    (e) day centre
    (f) day hospital
    (g) out-patient clinic
    (h) clubs or societies
    (i) meals-on-wheels
    (j) voluntary visitor or agency visitor
    (k) visitor for the blind
    (l) visitor for the deaf
    (m) church
    (n) occupational therapist
    (o) DHSS (supplementary benefit)
    (p) housing
    (q) any other official source of help.

III. AVAILABLE COMMUNITY SUPPORT
1 Who does the old person turn to first if things go wrong?

Give name, address, and telephone number of this person (chief carer).

How does he/she get in touch with them?

2 Is the behaviour or illness burdensome to the chief carer?

(Does it involve dirt, noise, unhygienic, or inconvenient behaviour? Does it endanger either the old person or others?)

Give details.

3 If the chief carer is a *relative*, how long (in months or years) have they been looking after the old person?

What help are they giving?

How regularly is the help given?

Why is the present behaviour burdensome?

What other competing responsibilities has the chief carer?

Give details.

4 If the chief carer is a *neighbour or friend*, how long have they been looking after the old person?

What help are they giving?

How far do they live from the old person's home?

Why is the present behaviour burdensome?

IV. ACTION TAKEN IF OLD PERSON REMAINS IN HIS/HER OWN HOME

A. *Direct help to old person*

Can the old person remain in the community if:

You or a named colleague visit regularly;

Medical treatment is available from her GP;

With the help of services listed under II 9;

If the chief carer is given relief and support in the form of help of special housing or aids and adaptations to present house or financial help (specify which).

Action How often are you or a colleague going to visit this elderly person? (Be realistic.)

What other help do you intend to mobilize?

B. *Support to chief carers*

If a close relative, can they maintain the present situation with help from:

(a) services listed under II 9

(b) regular visits by you or a named colleague

(c) with short-term admissions for the old person
(d) with the help of a part-time visitor or volunteer
(e) with suitable medical support services (specify)
(f) with day hospital, day centre or rehabilitative care
(g) if the chief carer knows your name, or a colleague's so that she can get help should the need arise (supply address, telephone number with extension, and advice on best time to call)
(h) with direct payment for services to chief carer
(i) with relief from the caring role delegated to someone else on a paid basis
(j) with suitable adaptations to the property or rehousing
(k) any other help available (specify).

Action What help do you plan to give this relative? (Be specific.)
If a neighbour, can they maintain the present situation with help from:
(a) services listed under II 9
(b) regular visits by you or a named colleague to the elderly person
(c) if the neighbour knows your name, address, telephone number with extension, and can get in touch with you (or a named colleague) if the situation gets beyond her.

Action What help do you plan to give this neighbour? (Be specific.)

V. PROPOSED ACTION IN MORE SERIOUS CASES

A. *Where the situation is a 'nuisance'*
Make clear to whom it is a nuisance.
(a) can the difficulty be reduced by medical treatment?
(b) can the situation be maintained by the use of the support services listed under II 9?
(c) can you or a colleague help by:
regular home visits;
making links with medical or social services;
by giving personal help and support to the chief carer or neighbour?
Action Describe what action you think should be taken. (Be specific.)

B. *Where the situation constitutes a health hazard or danger and the old person is so confused that they cannot make a rational decision*

(a) can the difficulty be reduced by medical treatment?
(b) can the situation be improved by the use of any of the support services listed under II 9?
(c) is the chief carer able to contain the situation with help from you?
(d) can you take any immediate steps to maintain this old person in her/his home?

If the answer to the last question is 'No', the choice lies between the following alternatives:

Either suggest that the old person goes to a local authority or voluntary Home for the present;

Or encourage the old person to go to hospital as a voluntary patient.

The following procedures will be used rarely.

Admission to hospital for observation for 28 days. (Application supported by two doctors, one of whom has special experience of mental disorders.) Section 25, Mental Health Act (1959).

Admission to hospital and treatment for up to a year. (Application giving reasons by two doctors.) Section 26, Mental Health Act (1959).

Emergency admission to hospital for 3 days. (Application by nearest relative or social worker supported by GP or other doctor.) Section 29, Mental Health Act (1959).

Admission to hospital for not more than 3 months. (For certain categories of old people who are living in insanitary conditions and not receiving proper care and attention.) Section 47, National Assistance Act (1948).

Admission to hospital for not more than 21 days. (For the same categories as above, in an emergency.) National Assistance (Amendment) Act (1951).

Action Describe what action should be taken, with brief reasons.

VI. CONTINUING CARE

After old person has gone into a Home or hospital

There is need for continuity of care after a person has gone into either a Home or hospital

If you are the known social worker, you have a responsibility to your elderly client to make sure that efforts are made to help him or her to return home if this is possible.

If you dealt with the emergency situation, you should link up with the appropriate area office, with social work hospital staff, or residential staff in the Home, to ensure that efforts are being made to help the old person to return to his or her home if this is possible.

Action Who will you contact to forward this plan? What action will you personally take? (Be specific.)

4(c) **Guidelines for communicating with elderly people**

1. Write in advance for an appointment. Introduce yourself and explain why you have come. Provide means of identification.
2. Make sure that the client can hear what you say.
3. Talk in a quiet place without background noise or distraction.
4. Speak clearly and keep to the point.
5. Speak directly to the old person unless she is too ill to answer you.
6. Allow plenty of time and do not rush.
7. Allow for low esteem and shyness in clients. They may behave truculently because they are uncertain of your interest or aggrieved at having to ask for help. Show forbearance.
8. Take full account of differences in experience, environment, and attitudes between you and an elderly client.
9. Avoid using technical terms, familiar to you but puzzling to your hearer.
10. Try to understand local vernacular expressions and if in doubt, ask what they mean. Be prepared to explain what *you* mean in simple, homely terms.
11. Supplement verbal communication by, where appropriate, a handshake, a look, or an encouraging murmur.
12. Write in bold, clear typescript or handwriting and try to express yourself in simple English.
13. Address your client by her proper name. Avoid language which might seem patronizing.
14. Listen carefully to all that an old person says. Try to recognize the nugget of truth as well as inconsistencies in her story.
15. Ask for confirmation from others but do not expect the whole truth from any one informant.

16. Be patient with the agitated and attempt to distract rather than to contradict.
17. Avoid appearing to confirm delusional or hallucinatory material.
18. Show approval and interest when the old person speaks rationally.
19. If the client's conversation is disorientated or deluded, encourage a lucid interval by talking about something which gave pleasure in her past life.
20. Show interest, patience, and warmth of response.

4(d) **Problems faced by carers and possible solutions**

Problems	Possible solution
(a) *Old person's behaviour*	
1. Sleep disturbance – caused by: Night wandering; Micturition; Shouting	Night watch Moderate dose of sedative Accessible commode/no late fluids/ medical treatment of urinary infections or congestive heart failure
2. Faecal incontinence	Treatment of impaction/retraining and increased mobility/ incontinence laundry service
3. Urinary incontinence	Laundry service
4. General immobility/inability to get on and off commode and in and out of bed	Low beds/handrails/accessible commode Help with toilet by community nurse/bath attendant
5. Dangerous irresponsibility	Advice on safety factors/relief to relative by volunteers including sitting-in service
6. Patients making excessive demands/complaining of physical symptoms/likely to do themselves harm	See solutions under 5 Counselling help
7. Characteristics of elderly mentally infirm	Need for description/advice on tactful handling/counselling

Problems	Possible solution
(b) *Carer's own limitations*	
1. Length of time relative has been caring for elderly mentally infirm person	Recognition that length of bearing burden is relevant/counselling
2. Age of relative	The elderly may be caring for the very elderly, reduced strength. Practical aids and services should be supplied
3. Mental and physical health of relative may be affected	The relative as well as the patient may need medical or psychiatric treatment
4. Insufficient strength for lifting/ back strain	Medical treatment/social aids
5. Embarrassment	Practical advice on looking after personal toilet of elderly parent
6. Identification with elderly mentally infirm person	Counselling help in coming to terms with relative's fear of their own possible deterioration
(c) *Environmental and social conditions*	
1. Restriction of social life	Voluntary visitors/grannie sitters/ night watch service/good companions help
2. Stairs	Bring bed downstairs/supply commode
3. Financial disadvantage	Advise on attendance allowance/ invalid care allowance and payment of relatives where applicable (see Appendix 3 for details)
4. Children in Family	Family counselling
5. Strain on Family	See 4. above and suggest day care/ hospital day care facilities/ holiday relief/intermittant admission to hospital/ where available

Problems	Possible solution

(d) *Admission of elderly mentally infirm
to institutional care*

1. In either local authority home of hospital

Liaise with residential and hospital social work staff/encourage relative to continue to visit old person regularly/keep contact with family during admission and after discharge

(e) *Helping the bereaved*

1. Bereavement

Practical help and advice on Will (see Appendix 2, dealing with practical matters relating to death/adjusting to changed circumstances/doing 'grief' work

Appendix 4(d) adapted and expanded from Sanford (1975).

4(e) **Helping to keep old people in the community**

Many mentally infirm old people manage to remain in the community because of the efforts of relatives, friends, and neighbours.

When you work with an old person as a client, do you know who is giving help and support? Who may be under unusual strain? Who, in addition to your primary client, may be in need of support and help?

Here are some questions which you might ask in such a situation.

1. Who is the person taking the chief responsibility for the old person? Name, address, telephone number.
2. Give circumstances or reasons which might make this key person unwilling to continue to care for the old person (e.g. physical disability, embarrassment, overcrowding, competing demands of other members of family, their increasing age, or infirmity, personality clashes, behaviour of old person, etc.).
3. What help or services would you plan to give the key relative so that they might continue to help the infirm old person?
4. What help and services would you offer to the old person so that she might remain under the care of the key relative? (e.g. meals-

185

on-wheels, home help, community nurse, day patient care, night sitters, home laundry, voluntary visitor. Advice about supplementary pension, exceptional needs grants, attendance allowance, etc., holiday relief, special aids, alterations to home, etc.).

5. Should the infirm old person go into short- or long-term institutional care how do you intend to keep in touch with relatives and what help will you still offer them? (e.g. acting as linkman with residential or hospital staff, recommending relatives group discussions, encouraging visits, and helping relatives to come to terms with death and bereavement. Practical help and advice.)

APPENDIX 5: KEY ADDRESSES

Age Concern
(National Old People's Welfare
Council),
Bernard Sunley House,
60 Pitcairn Road,
Mitcham,
Surrey CR4 3LL.
(01 640 5431).

Help the Aged,
32 Dover Street,
London W1.
(01 493 6515).

British Red Cross Society,
9 Grosvenor Crescent,
London SW1.
(01 235 5454).

Community Projects Foundation,
7 Leonard Street,
London EC2.
(01 251 0033).

Community Service Volunteers,
237 Pentonville Road,
London N1.
(01 278 6601).

Cruse,
126 Sheen Road,
Richmond, Surrey.
(01 940 4818).

International Voluntary Service,
53 Regent Road,
Leicester LE1 6YL.
(0533 541862).

National Association for Mental
Health,
(MIND),
22 Harley Street,
London W1.
(01 637 0741).

National Council of Social Service,
26 Bedford Square,
London WC1B 3HU.
(01 636 4066).

National Federation of
Old Age Pensions Associations,
91 Preston New Road,
Blackburn,
Lancs.
(0254 52606).

National Federation of Women's
Institutes,
39 Eccleston Street,
London SW1.
(01 730 7212).

Spastics Society,
12 Park Crescent,
London W1N 4EQ.
(01 636 5020).

187

Care of the Elderly Mentally Infirm

Task Force
1 Thorpe Close,
London W10.
(01 960 5669).

Toc H.,
1 Forest Close,
Wendover,
Aylesbury,
Bucks. HB22 6BT.
(0296 623911).

Women's Royal Voluntary
Services,
17 Old Park Lane,
London W1Y 4AJ.
(01 499 6040).

APPENDIX 6: VOLUNTARY SOCIAL SERVICES

Voluntary services for old people are often co-ordinated through local old people's welfare groups. Services which may be provided by the groups are:

Visiting

Advice and information

Individual services – shopping, reading aloud, gardening, decorating, hairdressing, escorting

Day centres

Lunch clubs

Good neighbour and street warden schemes

Emergency cash grants

Financial advice

Heating appliances

Social clubs

Mobile meals

Laundry

Chiropody

Transport by car, wheelchair, or special vehicle

Mobile libraries

Holidays

Employment and job finding

Exhibitions and competitions

Help in emergencies

Youth Help

Help with accommodation problems

Boarding out

Aids for the infirm

Day and night sitter-in services

Recruitment of workers

Courses and classes for workers and for the elderly

Conferences and meetings

Choir, drama, and hobbies festivals

Inter-club activities

Spiritual aspects

Education and research

Publicity

Radio and TV sets – provision and repair

Outings and entertainments

APPENDIX 7: MRS SARAH MERTON, AGED 87, A CLIENT AT RISK

personal and social circumstances	interpretations and possible actions to be considered
Mrs Sarah Merton, aged 87, an elderly widow and one of Dr Hazelhurst's patients.	Dr Hazelhurst, a local GP, telephones the area office of the Social Services Department. He reports that Mrs Merton will be at risk if she remains in her own home.
Miss Eileen Vesey, social worker at area office.	Referral allocated to Miss Vesey who has no prior knowledge of Mrs Merton. Miss Vesey consults the departmental register of old people, looks up local area records. No information available. Miss Vesey consults local health visitor and telephones Dr Hazelhurst. She asks for details about Mrs Merton's health and behaviour, whether the medical prognosis is hopeful and on what grounds he considers Mrs Merton is at risk. She telephones at about 11.15 a.m., a time she hopes will be convenient to the GP.
Dr Hazelhurst reports that Mrs Merton's mental state has declined steeply: in his view she is senile. He fears that she might have an accident through leaving on the gas, or fall downstairs in her nocturnal wanderings.	Dr Hazelhurst suggests Mrs Merton should be admitted to a local authority home, 'Sunnymede', where he knows there is an existing vacancy.

190

personal and social circumstances	*interpretations and possible actions to be considered*

	Miss Vesey promises to telephone Dr Hazelhurst with further information at a pre-arranged time. She fills in basic information on her assessment form (see Appendix 4(b)). She writes to Mrs Merton telling her that Dr Hazelhurst has asked her to call in case there is anything she can do to help. She suggests a time for her visit. Miss Vesey calls on Mrs Merton. She introduces herself and reminds her of the purpose of her visit. She asks whether Mrs Merton can manage and whether there is anyone who can give her a helping hand.
Mrs Merton seems pleased to see Miss Vesey. She asks her into the house which is in a terraced block in a busy street not far from the centre of town. The house is very cold. The back room, into which Miss Vesey is invited, is heated by a single bar of an electric fire. Mrs Merton is pale, painfully thin, dressed in two skirts, the shorter one on top of the longer one. Several scarves are pinned over layers of jumpers. Mrs Merton appears dejected and undernourished. She offers Miss Vesey a cup of tea but forgets to make one. Mrs Merton is eating some chicken soup from which she extracts fragments of meat which she explains she cannot swallow.	Mrs Merton may need advice about help with paying her electricity bill. The manner of dress is unusual. Mrs Merton may need advice on diet. How well is she eating?
Mrs Merton says she usually eats well, 'I have a chop and two veg.'	Miss Vesey asks her what she usually has for her main meal.

191

personal and social circumstances	*interpretations and possible actions to be considered*
Mrs Merton does not have meals-on-wheels at home but she says one of her neighbours, Mrs Claymore, usually does her shopping. She cooks her own meals. Mrs Merton shows the social worker over her house. The bed is in disarray, the stairs are very steep and in the kitchen a decaying kipper is stuck to the floor. There is a gas ring on the floor in the kitchen on which Mrs Merton boils her keetle; nearby is a threadbare mat which is stained with cooking fat. The house, though stale, is not dirty, and has been well kept until recently.	Miss Vesey asks whether Mrs Merton receives meals-on-wheels?
	If Mrs Merton agrees should a new safety cooker be installed? The mat is a fire risk – could it be replaced with lino?
Mrs Merton tells Miss Vesey that Mrs Roberts, a home help, calls on her once a week. Mrs Merton complains at intervals about her poor sight. 'It's like seeing clouds,' she says.	Miss Vesey asks whether Mrs Merton has any help in the home?
	Notes possible need for Mrs Merton to see optician. Ask Dr Hazelhurst? Is this cataract?
Mrs Merton explains that apart from Mrs Roberts she sees only one of her neighbours. She would turn to her in a crisis. Mrs Merton says she keeps herself to herself. She has a daughter, Susan, but she lives 'somewhere down south'. Mrs Merton's husband is dead and so are her two sons whose photographs stand on the sideboard.	Miss Vesey asks if a relative or a friend or a neighbour lives nearby and gives her help or companionship. Who does Mrs Merton go to if she feels ill? Find out daughter's name, address, and telephone number.
Mrs Merton is convinced that Miss Vesey is a friend of her daughter, Susan, despite Miss Vesey's efforts to explain who she really is. 'I'll tell Sue you called, she'll be glad I've seen you.'	Miss Vesey notes that Mrs Merton is confused about the social worker's identity. Explanations fail to clarify the situation.

personal and social circumstances	*interpretations and possible actions to be considered*

Remember me to your mother, a nice woman.'

Mrs Merton's manner is vague, but not otherwise peculiar. She seems to withdraw herself at times and does not always answer Miss Vesey's questions. She picks at her skirt in a depressed manner.

Miss Vesey is aware that Mrs Merton seems withdrawn and depressed. Depression or early stage of brain failure? Withdrawal at end of life?

Mrs Merton does not mind Miss Vesey calling on Mrs Claymore. She appears to lost interest in the remainder of what Miss Vesey says, though she brightens at the suggestion of more help in the house.

Miss Vesey asks if she may have a word with Mrs Merton's neighbour, Mrs Claymore. She says that she will ask Dr Hazelhurst if there is anything that can be done about Mrs Merton's poor sight and health generally. She asks if the old lady could do with some extra help in house? Would she like meals at home, if this could be arranged? Miss Vesey promises to call again on Friday to tell Mrs Merton what she has been able to arrange on her behalf.

Mrs Claymore, a widow of 72, has known Mrs Merton for over thirty years. She describes her elderly neighbour, 'a splendid strong-minded woman'. She has dealt courageously with all her problems, including the death of her sons during the war and her husband's death seven years previously. Her daughter, Susan, the weakling of the family lives fifty miles away and is unlikely to be of much support to her mother. Mrs Claymore says that Mrs Merton's health has been declining steadily for over six months. She is not eating properly, existing on toast, tea,

Miss Vesey calls on Mrs Claymore explaining the purpose of her visit.

It appears that Mrs Merton's decline is relatively recent.

Is Mrs Merton actually having a cooked dinner?

personal and social circumstances	*interpretations and possible actions to be considered*

and soup, and 'a bit of fish when I can get into town to buy it for her'. Mrs Merton wanders about at night and stands at her front door in the small hours staring into the street. She is absentminded with fires, gas-stoves, and water taps. Last spring a decorator, painting Mrs Merton's bedroom, found several pound notes pushed under the carpet. 'What if someone broke in and did the old lady harm?' Mrs Claymore says that her neighbour would not want to go and live with her daughter. She dislikes her son-in-law and values her independence.

Neighbour concerned about Mrs Merton's safety.

Apparently nearest relative will not be of immediate help and support.

Mrs Claymore is willing to keep an eye on her neighbour, to shop for her, and to deal with sickness or emergencies. She is on the telephone and she gives her number to Miss Vesey, receiving hers in exchange. Mrs Claymore is not prepared to take on more responsibility. Nothing has happened to Mrs Merton during the last year to account for her declining health.

Miss Vesey asks if Mrs Claymore can continue to give the help which she does at present to Mrs Merton?
Miss Vesey gives Mrs Claymore her name, address, and telephone number. If she is not available when Mrs Claymore phones, she will be contacted speedily by the duty officer and will make contact with Mrs Claymore at the earliest opportunity. Mrs Claymore an important link with the Social Services Department. May need reassurance. Miss Vesey notes that nothing unusual has happened which might account for Mrs Merton's decline in health.

Mrs Roberts is greatly concerned about Mrs Merton. Until recently her house was always bright and clean; now it is untidy and messy. Mrs Merton prefers her home help to talk to her instead of doing

Miss Vesey returns to her office, telephones the home help organizer, who puts her in touch with Mrs Roberts the home help.

194

personal and social circumstances	*interpretations and possible actions to be considered*

the housework. Mrs Merton is behaving queerly. She keeps confusing Mrs Roberts with her own daughter. She has let the house deteriorate from her previous high standards. She used to be a neat and tidy dresser and now always looks unkept and eccentric. She puts milk into the teapot instead of the cup when she prepares tea. Her conversation is confused at times. Mrs Roberts is afraid that one day she will go to the house and find that Mrs Merton has fallen downstairs. She will be willing to do more work for the old lady if her home help organizer can arrange it.

More evidence of decline in behaviour and standards of personal and home care.

Miss Vesey resolves to take up offer immediately. She telephones Dr Hazelhurst. He is aware of the eye problem. Mrs Merton has cataracts which are not yet ready for operation, supposing that she is strong enough to undertake one. He will consult Dr English the local geriatrician and ask him to examine Mrs Merton.

Please consult the assessment form (Appendix 4(b), pp. 176–82 and compose a brief diagnosis/prognosis on Dr English's behalf.

On this basis consider (as if you were Miss Vesey) what help and support you would offer to Mrs Merton:
(a) in the short term;
(b) in the long term.

APPENDIX 8: BRIEF CASE STUDIES FOR DISCUSSION

This Appendix should be read in conjunction with Appendix 4(e)
Consider what help and services you would like to make available to the following.

Miss Grant, a gentle, faded 58-year-old, who looks much older. Her mother is 82, has been bed-ridden for three years, incontinent for six months, and is mentally very confused. The doctor holds out no hope of her condition improving. Miss Grant, having given up her job, draws a dependent relative allowance. She copes with changing her mother, washing and drying the bed linen. She is immensely tired and dreads the future. She looks forward to her mother's death when she will be relieved of the everlasting chores. This provokes guilt and the reflection that she will then find herself alone, unemployed, and at a time of life when it is not easy to make new friends.

Mr and Mrs Redding, in the middle forties, with three adolescent children, live in a terraced house in a dilapidated neighbourhood. Mrs Lewis, aged 78, the mother of Mrs Redding, has lived with the family for over two years. She is a tiny, apparently docile little woman with an apologetic manner, but her daughter sees her as 'dirty and noisy, wandering about at night, in and out of the children's rooms. She never tries to help herself when she is ill.' She adds, 'My husband is at the end of his tether, he's threatened to walk out if I don't get rid of her.' Mrs Lewis sleeps upstairs and the only available WC is outside. Mrs Redding explodes with rage, 'You get her into hospital, and there she can stay. I don't want her back here again – ever.'

Mrs Fairlie, aged 87, went to stay for a short holiday with her son-in-law and daughter, Mr and Mrs Betts, aged 75 and 67 respectively. She fell ill with pneumonia, recovered from her physical symptoms but continued to show gross signs of brain failure. She was restive, agitated, and totally incontinent; at times, she was dependent, having to be supported from room to room, at other times creeping unaided down the steep stairs of the Betts' maisonette. She hid money, threw pots of flowers into the street, tore up the sleeves of records and managed to slash her daughter's favourite handbag. Mr and Mrs Betts had coped well with Mrs Fairlie's early illness and they sought to continue to give all the help they could. Mrs Betts, however, was a frail woman, normally a semi-invalid herself. She was frightened by her mother's manner which was occasionally wild and threatening, and she lost sleep because of her nocturnal wanderings. Mr Betts, an intelligent and energetic man, managed to organize a great many support services including a home help, a community nurse, and a laundry service. He took over the cooking and cleaning to free his wife to look after her mother. Nevertheless, Mrs Betts' health was under intolerable strain and within three months she collapsed exhausted. Mrs Fairlie was taken into the local hospital for observation. 'I feel so guilty,' said Mrs Betts, 'but I just can't go on.'

Mrs Celest, a gentle conscientious woman in her early sixties, who since her early twenties had helped her dominating mother, doing her washing and cleaning regularly, nursing her through periods of convalescence, and giving her regular holidays and treats. Mr Celest, though fond of his indomitable mother-in-law, was not willing to take over full responsibility for her. In his view his wife's brother who lived within a few hundred yards of the old lady should take equal responsibility. If he would take the old lady into his home for half the year, Mrs Celest would willingly do so for the other half. The brother refused to help and Mrs Celest continued to take a series of awkward bus journeys to visit her elderly mother even after her husband was taken into hospital. At this inopportune moment a new social worker began to visit the old lady and was very critical of Mrs Celest's efforts to cope with her confused and incontinent mother. After forty years of shouldering this heavy burden Mrs

197

Celest, who needed practical help herself, was made to feel like an uncaring daughter.

Vernon Parry was 72 years of age when, after forty years of happy married life, his wife Evelyn suddenly became ill. Her appearance and manner changed. She became unkempt and her conversation was incoherent and impetuous with intermittent lapses into withdrawn silences. She was unable to dress herself, attempting to pull a jumper over her legs. She followed her husband about pestering him with meaningless questions until he, the mildest of men, was afraid that he would lose his temper and speak sharply to her. Mr Parry had had a recent coronary; his doctor held out no hope of improvement in his wife's mental health. In the doctor's view Mr Parry should not continue to care for her. His daughter was not prepared to help; his friends' assistance was meagre, they were embarrassed by Evelyn's unpredictable, childlike behaviour. Vernon Parry coped unaided with his problem for six months when he died of a heart attack. Within thirty-six hours of his death his wife was placed in a nursing home.

Mr Coates, senior, a man of 85, was taken into hospital for a prostate gland operation. He had lived for seven years with his son and daughter-in-law and their two teenage children. In hospital he became argumentative and agitated. He failed to recognize his son and kept trying to climb out of bed despite his weak state. The hospital doctor was sure this period of confused behaviour was temporary and that it would clear up once the old man was restored to familiar surroundings. On returning home, his mental condition improved temporarily but it soon declined again. The GP arranged for the old man to be assessed at a psychogeriatric unit and the family discovered a place for him at a specialist day residential centre. Intermittent admissions were arranged so that this loyal but hard-pressed family could recoup and rest.

APPENDIX 9:
ADDITIONAL TABLES

Table 9   *Delivery of meals*
This table details the number of main meals served in recipients' homes and in clubs, centres, etc. in one sample week in England during November 1976. The figure for the number of meals served in recipients' homes is then broken down to show in more detail how this service was being used.

	served in own home	served in club etc.	total
number of main meals served	519,600	338,900	858,500
percentage of total	60·5%	39·5%	100%

number of persons served at home with

1 meal	2 meals	3 meals	4 meals	5 meals	6 meals	7 meals
13,000	74,800	20,300	13,700	31,700	2,900	5,000
(7·6%)	(43·6%)	(17·7%)	(8·0%)	(18·5%)	(1·7%)	(2·9%)

Adapted from DHSS (1977).

Table 10   *Aids to households*
In 1976, 317,200 households received aids through local authority assistance (excluding those receiving assistance with adaptations to property, and holidays). *Table 10* outlines the forms that this assistance took, and the number of households (covering all ages) in England receiving particular forms of aid.

installed telephone	rentals	supplied installed TV	annual TV licence	supplied radio	other aids	adapted property	holidays
14,800	69,000	1,600	38,500	500	191,200	48,600	101,400

Adapted from DHSS (1977c).

Table 11 *Persons in residential accommodation who are aged 65 and over, and who are aged 65 and over and mentally disordered. England, 1975 and 1976 (1976 figures in brackets)*

	residential accommodation provided by or on behalf of local authorities	registered voluntary homes	registered private homes	total
aged 65 and over				
men	30,750 (31,837)	—	—	—
women	78,993 (83,274)	—	—	—
both	109,743 (115,111)	22,454 (23,788)	18,759 (21,320)	150,955 (160,219)
aged 65 and over mentally disordered	18,831 (21,320)	207 (222)	259 (317)	19,297 (21,859)

Adapted from DHSS 1977.

Table 12 *Persons in residential accommodation (all ages) by size of home. England, 1970, 1975, and 1976*

year	bed complement under 31 beds	31–50 beds	51–70 beds	71–150 beds	over 150 beds	total
1970	11,292	41,068	22,641	9,023	4,702	88,726
1975	10,834	51,887	28,052	6,968	1,668	99,409
1976	10,570	55,415		37,503		103,488

Adapted from DHSS (1977).

GLOSSARY

ACUTE BRAIN SYNDROME An American term for a confusional state of recent origin which is usually due to organic illness elsewhere in the body. The equivalent expression used in this book is 'extrinsic brain failure'.

AFFECTIVE DISORDER Disturbance of the emotions rather than of the intellect, e.g. depression.

ALZHEIMER'S DISEASE This is the commonest cause of dementia or brain failure in later life. The condition is characterized by specific pathological changes spread diffusely throughout the brain, usually commencing in late middle age and becoming clinically manifest in late old age. In a few cases in which clinical advance of brain failure is evident before the age of 60, the condition is known as 'pre-senile dementia'.

ANXIETY STATE A prolonged or recurrent disorder in which anxiety is disproportionate to its apparent cause.

ARTERIOSCLEROSIS (more properly called ATHEROSCLEROSIS) Pathological narrowing of the medium- and large-sized arteries with ulceration and thrombus formation, leading to progressive damage of the tissues served by the diseased arteries.

ARTERIOSCLEROTIC DEMENTIA This term is widely used to describe the common condition of intellectual impairment resulting from progressive damage to the brain as a result of disease of blood vessels. The damage takes the form of multiple small haemorrhages or blood clots scattered throughout the brain. In this book the term 'vascular brain failure' replaces 'arteriosclerotic dementia'.

BRAIN FAILURE This is a general term used to describe impairment of the function of the brain from whatever cause, other than the distinct presence of a discrete focal lesion such as a brain tumour. Brain failure is divided into two main groups: intrinsic brain failure in which the brain fails because of diffuse disease of its own tissues; and extrinsic brain failure in which the brain fails because of disease outside the brain acting upon it. The onset of brain failure may be insidious or sudden; and its manifestations may be mild, moderate, or severe.

CEREBRAL ARTERIOSCLEROSIS This term properly means atherosclerosis of the larger blood vessels supplying the brain. It is widely, but not strictly correctly, used as being equivalent to brain failure caused by multiple infarcts in the brain, for which the term 'vascular brain failure' is preferred.

CHRONIC BRAIN SYNDROME This is synonymous with brain failure, however caused, of insidious onset.

COGNITIVE DISTURBANCE A disturbance of the intellectual processes.

CONFUSION This word is used to describe any intellectual disturbance in the elderly, including disorientation for time, place, and persons, memory impairment, delusions, hallucinations, and abnormal behaviour. Confusion is a symptom of many diseases and not a disease in itself. The term has been largely avoided in this book.

CONFUSIONAL STATE Illness of recent onset characterized by disturbances of thought processes. A confusional state is generally induced by a disease outside the brain; the condition is thus the same as 'extrinsic brain failure'.

DELIRIUM This condition is characterized by clouding of consciousness and may be accompanied by disorientation, delusions, hallucinations, fear, and disordered behaviour. Delirium is usually a manifestation of extrinsic brain failure.

DELUSIONS These are irrational beliefs or systems of belief which may be held with great tenacity or which may be transient, and are a feature of brain failure, depression, and other psychiatric disturbances.

DEMENTIA This term implies impairment of intellectual function usually as a result of structural disease of the brain. The term is thus equivalent to intrinsic brain failure. The word 'dementia' is sometimes used to describe extrinsic brain failure when this is of gradual onset, or when its nature is not clearly understood. Unfortunately some of the older definitions of 'dementia' include the term 'irreversible' in it. Regrettably this has led to the impression that 'dementia' is always untreatable. It is for this reason amongst others that the term dementia has been largely replaced in this book by the alternative expression 'brain failure' which carries no such connotation.

DEPRESSION In common parlance this means a mood of sadness, whereas in psychiatry depression is the name of a severe emotional illness whose clinical features usually but not invariably include sadness. The definition of depression in the elderly is particularly difficult (see pp.31–2).

DIOGENES SYNDROME This expression was coined to describe cases of total social breakdown characterized by self-neglect and abandonment of cleanliness and order, in the absence of significant physical or mental illness. The term should not be applied to patients who are unable to care for themselves because of physical illness, dementia, or depression.

DISORIENTATION Loss of accurate awareness of time and place, usually but not invariably accompanied by fluctuating delusions of incorrect time and place.

EARNINGS RULE After pensionable age, women under 65 and men under 70 who go on working and earn more than £52.10 a week, lose a proportion of their pension for anything that they earn above that sum. At 65 women, and at 75 men, can draw their full pension without restriction on (taxable) earnings. (Figures correct at November 1979.)

EMI Elderly mentally infirm.

ESMI Elderly with severe mental infirmity.

GRADUATE This term was coined to describe elderly patients in mental hospitals who had been admitted earlier in life and remained in hospital until they entered old age. The majority of these patients are schizophrenics.

HALLUCINATION A sensory experience not based on external reality. The experience may be auditory, i.e. hearing voices which are not there; visual, i.e. seeing people; or they may be based on any of the other senses. 'Hallucinosis' is the tendency to recurrent hallucinations.

HOUSEHOLD One person living alone or a group of people living at the same address having meals prepared together and with common housekeeping.

HOSPICE Home for the destitute, sick, or dying.

HYPOCHONDRIASIS Recurrent delusions of ill health, not based on reality. Hypochondriasis is often a symptom of depression.

HYPOMANIA A state of abnormal excitement or elation equivalent to mania. This sometimes alternates with depression.

IATROGENIC This means 'caused by medicine' or 'caused by the doctor'. Iatrogenic illness is often produced by drugs given for the treatment of another condition.

INFARCT An area of dead tissue caused by a haemorrhage or blood clot interfering with the blood supply of the part.

LATE PARAPHRENIA This is an illness coming on in late life characterized by self-imposed isolation, emotional coldness, self-neglect, and mild paranoid delusions.

LESION A general word for damaged tissue, however caused.

LESSER ELIGIBILITY The situation of the able-bodied poor in a workhouse should be inferior to that of an independent labourer of the lowest class in the community.

MANIA A state of severe excitement or elation, possibly accompanied by violence, and often ending in utter exhaustion.

MANIC-DEPRESSIVE PSYCHOSIS A life-long disease characterized by alternating periods of depression and hypomania with intervals of normal health.

MULTI-INFARCT DEMENTIA A recently introduced term which has the same connotation as 'arteriosclerotic dementia' and 'vascular brain failure'.

NEUROSIS An emotional disturbance in a person of susceptible personality not based on structural abnormality in the brain and not conforming to the pattern of a major psychiatric illness.

NON-VERBAL COMMUNICATION Expressions and gestures which give a clue to the underlying attitude of individuals.

OBSESSION A fixed delusion which dominates consciousness and determines behaviour, often of a ritualistic type.

PARANOIA A fixed delusion or system of delusions characterized by a vivid sense of the hostility of part or all of the outside world and a sense of persecution.

PERSONALITY DISORDER A life-long pattern of abnormal or anti-social behaviour, not due to disease or to environmental constraints.

PSYCHOSIS A major psychiatric illness with a characteristic phenomenological pattern, e.g. manic-depressive illness, schizophrenia.

RETIRED PEOPLE All those not working who have reached pensionable age.

SCHIZOPHRENIA A major mental illness of adult life characterized by disordered concepts of reality.

SENILE DEMENTIA A widely used expression, but one which is not employed in this book. The term is used to describe any form of intellectual deficit in old age, but is also used to refer specifically to Alzheimer's Disease occurring in subjects after the age of 60, in contrast to vascular brain failure.

SENILITY This lay expression is not recommended for professional use. It implies a general state of physical, mental, and social degeneration, rather than a specific diagnostic category.

SENIUM This means old age, not precisely defined, but carries the implication that it is the period of life in which intellectual breakdown is likely to occur.

VASCULAR Related to blood vessels.

Vascular brain failure means loss of brain tissue secondary to disease of the supplying blood vessels.

WORKHOUSE TEST The able-bodied poor should only be given relief if they consented to enter a workhouse.

REFERENCES

ABEL-SMITH, B. and TOWNSEND, P. (1965) *The Poor and the Poorest.* London: Bell.

ABRAMS, M. (1978) *Beyond Three-Score and Ten.* Mitcham: Age Concern Research Publication.

AGE CONCERN (1973) *Visiting Organiser's Guide.* Mitcham: Age Concern Publications.

—— (1974) *Accommodation for the Elderly.* Mitcham: Age Concern Publications.

—— (1977) *Building for Our Future, Housing Problems of the Elderly – A Prescription for Change.* Mitcham: Age Concern Publications.

AGE CONCERN RESEARCH UNIT (1977) *Profiles of the Elderly. Volume 1.* Mitcham: Age Concern Publications.

—— (1977a) *Profiles of the Elderly. Volume 2.* Mitcham: Age Concern Publications.

ANDREWS, J. (1972) The future of the psycho-geriatric patient. In British Hospital Journal and Kings Fund Hospital Centre (Sponsors) *The Elderly Mind.* London: British Hospital Journal.

ANDREWS, C. (1975) Career Grade Working Party Report. *British Association of Social Workers News* (24 July).

BARNES, E. K., SACK, A., and SHORE, H. Guidelines to treatment approaches, modalities and methods for use with the aged. *The Gerontologist* 13: 513–27.

BAYLEY, M. (1973) *Mental Handicap and Community Care.* London: Routledge and Kegan Paul.

BELL, C. R. (1968) *Middle Class Families.* London: Routledge and Kegan Paul.

BENJAMIN, A. (1969) *The Helping Interview.* Boston: Houghton Mifflin.

BENNETT, A. (1911) *Clayhanger.* Harmondsworth: Penguin (1970: 361).

BERGMAN, K. (1973) Letter. *New Society* 22: 531.

BEVERIDGE, W. E. (1965) How Worthwhile is Retirement? *New Society* (June).

206

BIGOT, A. (1970) *Apathy among elderly people living in Residential Homes.* (An interim report and working paper.) University of Nottingham.

BLAIR, B., CONSTABLE, D., and DAVIES, P. (1975) *Caring for the Confused Elderly.* (Advisory Team EMI Project.) Cheshire Social Services Department.

BLAU, Z. S. (1973) *Old Age in a Changing Society.* New York: New Viewpoint.

BOLDY, D., ABEL, P., and CARTER, K. (1973) *The Elderly in Grouped Dwellings, A Profile.* Exeter: University of Exeter.

BOSANQUET, N. (1975) *New Deal for the Elderly.* London: Fabian Society.

BREARLEY, C. P. (1975) *Social Work, Ageing and Society.* London: Routledge and Kegan Paul.

―― (1977) *Residential Work with the Elderly.* London: Routledge and Kegan Paul.

BREE, M. H. (1960) *The Dement in the Community.* Oxford: Horton Group, H.M.C.

BRITISH ASSOCIATION OF SOCIAL WORKERS (1977) Social work with the elderly. *Social Work Today* (12 April).

BROMLEY, D. B. (1974) *The Psychology of Human Ageing.* 2nd edition. Harmondsworth: Penguin.

BUMAGIN, V. E. (1972) Challenge of working with old people. *Social Work Today* (14 December).

BUTTERWORTH, E. and HOLMAN, R. (1975) *Social Welfare in Modern Britain.* Glasgow: Fontana.

CANVIN, R. and PEARSON, N. (eds) (1973) *Needs of the Elderly.* Exeter: University of Exeter.

CARSTAIRS, V. and MORRISON, M. (1971) *The Elderly in Residential Care.* Scottish Home & Health Department, (Health Service Studies No. 19). Edinburgh: HMSO.

CARTWRIGHT, A., HOCKEY, L., and ANDERSON, J. *Life Before Death.* London: Routledge and Kegan Paul.

CENTRAL OFFICE OF INFORMATION (1977) *Care of the Elderly in Britain* (Pamphlet 121). London: HMSO.

CENTRAL STATISTICAL OFFICE (1976) *Annual Abstract of Statistics.* London: HMSO.

―― (1976a) *Social Trends no. 7.* London: HMSO.

―― (1977) *Social Trends no. 8.* London: HMSO.

CHARTERED INSTITUTE OF PUBLIC FINANCE AND ACCOUNTANCY (1974) *Local Health & Social Service Statistics 1972/3.* London: CIPFA.

COHEN, R. (1957) Casework with older persons. *Social Work* 2: 30–5.

COLE, D. and UTTING, J. (1962) *The Economic Circumstances of Old People.* London: Codicote.

COLWELL, C. and POST, F. (1959) Community needs of elderly psychiatric patients. *British Medical Journal* 2: 214–17.

COMMITTEE OF INQUIRY INTO THE IMPACT OF RATES ON HOUSE-HOLDS (1965) Cmnd. 2582. London: HMSO.

CONNOLLY, J. (1962) The social and medical circumstances of old people admitted to a psychiatric hospital. *Medical Officer* (10 August).

CORSELLIS, J. A. N. (1962) *Mental Illness and the Ageing Brain*. London: Oxford University Press.

CREER, C. and WING, J. (1974) *Schizophrenia at Home*. Surbiton Report of National Schizophrenia Fellowship. (May.)

CRESSWELL, J. *et al.* (1972) *New Society* **20**: 410.

CROSS, C. (ed.) (1974) *Interviewing and Communication in Social Work*. London: Routledge and Kegan Paul.

CUMMING, E. and HENRY, W. E. (1961) *Growing Old: the Process of Disengagement*. New York: Basic Books.

DAVIS, L. *et al.* (1974) Meals on wheels deliveries. *Modern Geriatrics* **4**: 220.

DEPARTMENT OF EMPLOYMENT (1977) *Family Expenditure Survey*. London: HMSO.

DEPARTMENT OF HEALTH AND SOCIAL SECURITY (1970) *Psychiatric Assessment Unit*, Circular HM (70) 11: London: HMSO.

—— (1971) *Better Services for the Mentally Handicapped*. London: HMSO.

—— (1971a) *Services for Mental Illness Related to Old Age*, Circular HM (72) 71. London: HMSO.

—— (1971b) Circular 19, 29 March. London: HMSO.

—— (1973) *Building Note no. 2*. London: HMSO.

—— (1975) *Better Services for the Mentally Ill*. London: HMSO.

—— (1977) *Health and Personal Social Services Statistics for England* London: HMSO.

—— (1978) *Social Service Teams: The Practitioners' View*. London: HMSO.

—— (1978a) *Review of the Mental Health Act, 1959*, Cmnd. 7320. London: HMSO.

DOWDELL, T. C. (1976) *The Role of the Social Services in the Care of the Elderly Sick*. London: Socialist Medical Association.

EXTON-SMITH, A. and GRIMLEY EVANS, J. (1977) *Care of the Elderly*. London: Academic Press.

GARRETT, A. (1972) *Interviewing: its Principles and Methods*. New York: Family Service Association.

GIBBERD, K. (1977) *Residential Care, What Alternatives?* Mitcham: Age Concern Publications.

GOLDBERG, E. M. (1970) *Helping the Aged*. London: Allen and Unwin.

GOLDSMITH, V. (1975) Why can't a home be more like the real thing? *General Practitioner* (21 February).

GRAD, J. and SAINSBURY, P. (1966) Problems of caring for the mentally ill at home. *Proceedings of the Royal Society of Medicine* **59**: 20–30.

—— (1968) The effects that patients have on their families in a community care and a central psychiatric service – a two year follow-up. *British Journal of Psychiatry* **114**: 265–78.

GRANT, I. (1959) The Geriatric Question and Problems in Great Britain. *New Zealand Medical Journal* 58: issue no. 325 (June).

GRAY, M. (1978) The myth of objective assessment. *Community Care* (1 March).

GREEN, H. (1972) *I Never Promised You a Rose Garden*. London: Pan Books.

GREGORY, P. and YOUNG, M. (1972) *Lifeline Telephone Services for the Elderly*. Hull: National Innovations Centre.

GRIMLEY EVANS, J. (1975) The Elderly: Demography and Medical Needs. Paper read at the conference of the Royal College of Physicians (18 November).

—— (1979) Fractured Proximal Femur in Newcastle-upon-Tyne. *Age and Ageing* 8: 16–24.

GOWERS, E. (1948) *Plain Words*. London: HMSO.

HARRIS, A. (1968) *Social Work for the Elderly*. London: HMSO.

HENDRICKS, J. and HENDRICKS, C. D. (1977) *Ageing in Mass Society: Myths and Realities*. Cambridge, Mass.: Winthrop.

HERON, A. and CHOWN, S. M. (1967) *Age and Function*. Oxford: Churchill.

HOLMAN, R. (ed.) (1970) *Socially Deprived Families in Britain*. London: Bedford Square Press.

HUNT, A. (1978) *The Elderly at Home*. London: Office of Population Censuses and Surveys, HMSO.

INGLIS, B. (1971) *Poverty and the Industrial Revolution*. London: Hodder and Stoughton.

INSTITUTE OF ACTUARIES (1958) *Journal of the Institute of Actuaries* 84: 77.

ISAACS, B. (1971) Geriatric patients, do their families care? *British Medical Journal* 4: 282.

ISAACS, B., LIVINGSTONE, M., and NEVILLE, Y. (1972) *Survival of the Unfittest*. London: Routledge and Kegan Paul.

ISAACS, B. and CAIRD, F. A. (1976) Brain failure: A contribution to the terminology of mental abnormality in old age. *Age and Ageing* 5: 241–4.

JOLLEY, D. (1977) Hospital in-patient services for patients with dementia. *British Medical Journal* 1: 1335–6.

JOSLING, J. F. (1976) *Powers of Attorney* 4th edition. London: Oyez.

KADUSHIN, A. (1972) *The Social Work Interview*. New York: Columbia University Press.

KAY, D. W. K. (1963) Late paraphrenia and its bearing on the aetiology of schizophrenia. *Acta Psychiatrica Scandinavica* 39: 159–69.

KAY, D. W. K., BEAMISH, P., and ROTH, M. (1964) Old age mental disorders in Newcastle upon Tyne. *British Journal of Psychiatry* 110: 146–58; 668–82.

—— (1965) Old age mental disorders in Newcastle upon Tyne. *British Journal of Psychiatry* 111: 938–46.

KIDD, C. D. (1962) Misplacement of the elderly in hospital. *British Medical Journal* 2: 1491–3.

KINSEY, A. *et al.* (1949) *Sexual Behaviour in the Human Male.* Philadelphia: Saunders.

KOMAROVSKY, M. (1967) *Blue Collar Marriage.* New York: Random House.

KUSHLICK, A., FELCE, D., PALMER, J., and SMITH, D. *Evidence to the Committee of Inquiry into Mental Handicap, Nursing and Care.* Winchester: Health Care Evaluation Research Team.

MARSTON, N., and GUPTA, H. (1977) Interesting the old. *Community Care* (16 November).

MEACHER, M. (1972) *Taken for a Ride.* London: Longman.

MEZEY, A. G., HODKINSON, H. M., and EVANS, G. J. (1968) The elderly in their own unit. *British Medical Journal* 3: 17–19.

MIND (1973) *Psychogeriatric Services – the Questions Answered?* (Report No. 9.) London: National Association for Mental Health.

—— (1979) *Positive Approaches to Mental Infirmity in Elderly People.* (Annual Conference Report.) London: National Association for Mental Health.

MINISTRY OF HEALTH (1957) *H.M. (57) 86.* (Circular 14). London: HMSO.

MINISTRY OF HOUSING AND LOCAL GOVERNMENT AND THE WELSH OFFICE (1969) *Council House Purposes, Procedures and Priorities.* London: HMSO.

NATIONAL COUNCIL FOR THE SINGLE WOMAN AND HER DEPENDANTS (1973) *Financial Hardship and the Single Woman.* London: NCSWD.

OFFICE OF POPULATION CENSUSES AND SURVEYS (1974) *Census 1971 Great Britain Age, Marital Condition and General Tables.* London: HMSO.

—— (1976) *Population Estimates Series PP1 No. 1.* London: HMSO.

—— (1976a) *Population Projections No. 5. Census of Population Reports.* London: HMSO.

—— (1976b) *Variant Population Projections 1974–2011. Series PP2 No. 6.* London: HMSO.

OPIT, L. J. (1977) Domiciliary care for the elderly sick – economy or neglect? *British Medical Journal* 1: 30–3.

OWEN, D. (1976) *In Sickness and in Health – the Politics of Medicine.* London: Quartet Books.

PARKER, J. (1965) *Local Health and Welfare Services.* London: Allen & Unwin.

PARNELL, R. (1968) Prospective geriatric bed requirements in a mental hospital. *Gerontologia Clinica* 10: 30–6.

PARSONS, P. L. (1965) Mental health of Swansea's old folk. *British Journal of Preventive Social Medicine* 19: 43.

PERSONAL SOCIAL SERVICES COUNCIL (1978) *Residential Care Reviewed.* London: PSSC.

POST, F. (1944) Some problems arising from a study of mental patients over the age of 60 years. *Journal of Mental Science* **90**: 554–65.

POWELL, C. (1975) Caring for the relatives of the elderly. *Social Work Today* **6**: 228 (10 July).

RANSOME, H. (1978) *A study of the potential role of physiotherapy in Residential Part 3 Homes for the Elderly.* Greenwich Hospital.

REICHARD, S., LIVSON, F., and PETERSEN, P. G. (1962) *Ageing and Personality: A Study of Eighty-Seven Older Men.* New York: Wiley.

Report of the Committee on Local Authority and Allied Personal Social Services (Seebohm Report) (1968) Cmnd. 3703. London: HMSO.

Report by a Working Party on the Social Work (Scotland) Act. (1968) *Social Work in Scotland.* Edinburgh: University of Edinburgh.

RICH, J. (1968) *Interviewing Children and Adolescents.* London: Macmillan.

ROSS, D., and KREITMAN, N. (1975) A further investigation of differences in the suicide rates of England and Wales and of Scotland. *British Journal of Psychiatry* **127**: 572–82.

ROSSER, C. and HARRIS, C. (1965) *The Family and Social Change.* London: Routledge and Kegan Paul.

ROWLINGS, C. (1979) *Social Work with the Elderly: Some Problems and Possibilities.* London: Allen & Unwin.

ROWNTREE, B. S. (1947) *Old People.* London: Oxford University Press.

ROYAL COLLEGE OF GENERAL PRACTITIONERS (1978) Some suggestions for teaching co-operation between social work and general practice. *Journal of the Royal College of General Practitioners* **28**: 670.

SAINSBURY, P. (1960) *Report to the Conference on the Epidemiology of Mental Disorders.* Oxford: Nuffield Provincial Hospitals Trust.

—— (1968) Suicide and depression. In Coppen A. and Walk A. (eds) *British Journal of Psychiatry, Special Publication No. 2.*

SAINSBURY, P., and GRAD, J. (1966) Evaluating the community psychiatric service in Chichester. *Millbank Memorial Fund Quarterly* (January).

SANFORD, J. (1975) Tolerance of debility in elderly dependents by supporters at home. Its significance for hospital practice. *British Medical Journal* **3**: 471–3.

SAVAGE, R. D., BRITTON, P. G., BOTHAM, N., and HALL, E. H. (1973) *Intellectual Functioning in the Aged.* London: Methuen.

SCHWEINITZ, D. (1962) *Interviewing in the Social Services.* London: National Institute of Social Work.

SEAGRAVE, J. (1975) Coping with the OLD Explosion. *Community Care* (11 January).

SHANAS, E., TOWNSEND, P., WEDDERBURN, D., FRIIS, H., MILKAJ, A., and STEHOWER, J. (1968) *Old People in Three Industrial Societies.* London: Routledge and Kegan Paul.

SHELDON, J. H. (1948) *Social Medicine of Old Age.* London: Oxford University Press.

211

SIMOS, B. (1973) Adult Children and their Ageing Parents. *Social Work* (USA) **78** (May).

STEPHENSON, O. (1978) *Ageing: a professional perspective.* (Occasional Papers.) Mitcham: Age Concern Publications.

STOKOE, I. (1965) The physical and mental care of the elderly at home. In World Psychiatric Organization, *Psychiatric Disorders of the Aged.* Manchester: Geigy UK.

SUPPLEMENTARY BENEFITS COMMISSION (1976) *Annual Report* (Cmnd. 6910). London: HMSO.

TALLAND, J. A. (1968) *Disorders of Memory and Learning.* Harmondsworth: Penguin.

THOMPSON, A. P. (1949) Problems of ageing and chronic sickness. *British Medical Journal* **2**: 243–50; 300–05.

TOMLINSON, B. E. (1977) Morphological changes and dementia in old age. In Smith, L. W. and Kinsbourne, M. (eds) *Aging and Dementia.* New York: Spectrum.

TORRIE, M. (1975) *Begin Again.* London: Dent.

TOWNSEND, P. (1963) *The Family Life of Old People.* Harmondsworth: Penguin.

TOWNSEND, P. and WEDDERBURN, D. (1965) *The Aged in the Welfare State.* London: Bell.

TUNSTALL, J. (1966) *Old and Alone.* London: Routledge and Kegan Paul.

WAGER, R. (1972) *Care of the Elderly.* London: Institute of Municipal Treasurers and Accountants.

WELFORD, A. T. (1975) *Motivation, Capacity, Learning and Age.* Proceedings of the 10th International Congress of Gerontology.

WHELAN, M. and BREE, M. (1946) Conducing to the cure. Social psychiatry in the treatment of neuro syphilis by induced malaria. *Lancet* **2**: 477 (5 October).

—— (1954) Clinical outcome in treatment of G.P.I. and taboparesis. *Lancet* **1**: 70 (9 January).

WHITEHEAD, A. (1970) *In the Service of Old Age.* Harmondsworth: Penguin.

WHITTON, J. (1976) Conspiracy against a truly caring system for the elderly. *Health and Social Service Journal* (7 December).

—— (1977) How to quench the last flames of independence in old age. *Health and Social Service Journal* (3 June).

WILKES, R. *A Further Report on the Needs of Old People in Worcester.* (Report for the City of Worcester Health Department.) Undated.

WILLIAMS, M. (1970) *Brain Damage and the Mind.* Harmondsworth: Penguin.

WILLIAMSON, J., STOKOE, I. H., GRAY, S., FISHER, M., SMITH, A., MCGHEE, A., and STEPHENSON, P. H. (1964) Old people at home: their unreported needs. *Lancet* **1**: 1117–20.

WILLMOTT, P. (1967) *Consumer's Guide to the British Social Services.* Harmondsworth: Penguin.

WILLMOTT, P., and YOUNG, M. (1967) *Family and Class in a London Suburb.* London: New English Library.

WORLD HEALTH ORGANIZATION (1963) *Annual Epidemiological and Vital Statistics.* Geneva: WHO.

—— (1972) *World Health Statistics Annual: Volume 1.* Geneva: WHO.

WROE, D. C. L. (1973) *The Elderly. Social Trends.* London: HMSO.

INDEX

INDEX

Abscess, of the brain 10
Abstraction 23
Activity theory, of ageing 44
Admission to hospital, compulsory
    126 ff., 166 ff.
Admission to long-term care 144
'Adopt a Grannie' 93
Affective disorders 30 ff.
Age Concern 91
Ageing, theories of 44
Agitation 33, 109
Aids and appliances 86, 199
Alarm system 93
Alcohol 13, 35, 40, 41
Alzheimer's disease 12
Anxiety 14, 31
Appetite, loss of 32
Area team 83
Arteriosclerosis (Atherosclerosis) 9
    research into 147
Assessment 153, 175, 176 ff.
    Unit 155
Attendance allowance 172

'Bakewell club' 94
Behavioural treatment 38, 93
Bereavement 31, 93, 145
    and suicide 35
Bladder function 13
Blind Welfare Services 88
Blindness 6, 38, 108
Blood pressure, control of, 148
Boarding out 91
Body language 108

Bowel function 13
Brain failure 9 ff.
    symptoms 16 ff.
    extrinsic 10, 13, 174
    intrinsic 10, 12, 17, 174
    management 18 ff., 28
    non-vascular 10, 11
    research 147
    tests 27
    vascular 10, 11
Brain mechanisms 22 ff.
British Association of Social Workers
    158
British Geriatrics Society 157

Car help service 94
'Care Unlimited' 93
Careers
    help for 142
    limitations of 138
    problems 183
    solutions 183
Catchment areas 53, 60
Central Council for Education and
    Training in Social Work 158
Cerebral arteriosclerosis 9
Charities 89
Chiropody 87
Chronically Sick and Disabled Persons
    Act, 1970 82
Cleaning a home 120
Clouding of consciousness 13, 33
Colwell, Maria 109
Coma 13

217

Communication 101 ff.
Community nurse 49, 59
Community physician 166
Community services 84
Compulsory admission to hospital
126 ff., 166, 167
Compulsory removal from home 82,
126 ff., 166
Concentration, loss of,
in brain failure 6
in depression 32
Confabulation,
in brain failure 19, 24
in alcoholism 40
Confusion 8, 9, 109
Confusional state 10
Constipation 21
Convalescence 156
Coroner 35
Counselling of relatives 78, 138, 142
Court of Protection 169
Crisis intervention 122
'Crossroads Care Attendants Scheme'
92
Cross-sectional studies 7
'Cruse' 93

Day care 142
Day Centre 29, 89
Day hospital 52
for mentally infirm elderly 59
Deafness, services 6, 38, 108
Death 88
of pet 2
of spouse 2, 31
Delirium 13
Delusions 9, 13, 108
in depression 34
in paranoia 39
in paraphrenia 37
Dementia 9, 10
arteriosclerotic 11
senile 11
senile requirements 55
Demography 62 ff.
Denial 18, 19, 25
Department of Health and Social
Security (DHSS) 5, 55
Dependence 71, 136
Depression 6, 19, 31, 149
agitation 33
endogenous 32

manic-depressive psychosis 33
reactive 31
treatment 34
Diagnosis 114
Digit reversal test 27
Discharge from hospital 120, 143
Discrimination 23
Disengagement theory 44
Disorientation 9, 33
Diurnal rhythm 26
Domiciliary services 162
Drowsiness 13
Drugs 13
anti-depressant 34
dependence 40

'Easy Alert' 90
Elderly Mentally Infirm (EMI) 5
Elderly Severely Mentally Infirm
(ESMI) 5
Electroconvulsive Therapy (ECT) 34
Emotional disorders 13
Emotional lability 40
Employment 64
Errors 3, 16
Exchange system 156
Expenditure
of old people 75
in care of elderly 149
Experiments in community services
90 ff.

Family community care 91
Family
contact 70
size 67
Fire-risk 2
'Fish Scheme' 90
Flight of ideas 76
'Floating bed' 120, 142
Fluctuation
of intellect 25
of mood 33
'Flying Angels' 92
'Food-and-Friendship' service 94
Fostering 91
Freedom of the individual 125
Funerals 163

General Practitioner 49, 114
Geriatric medicine
departments 50
resources 52

Geriatric units 55, 154
Geriatricians 115, 157
Gesture 106
'Good Companions' 91
'Good Neighbour Scheme' 91
'Grannie's Help' 94
Grief 145
Group dwellings 96
Guidelines for Post-Qualifying Studies
     158
*Guidelines for Social Work with the
     Elderly* 158
Guilt feelings 33

Hallucinations 13, 108
  in paraphrenia 37
Health Services and Public Health Act,
     1968 81, 95, 162, 165
Health visitor 49
Hearing aid 108
Holiday relief 78, 142, 143
Home Help Service 84
Homicide 41
Hospices 93
Hospital services, statutory provisions
     165
Household composition 68
Housing 72, 78, 141
Hypochondria 32, 33
Hypomania 36

Income
  of old people 73
  of relatives 141
Incompatibility 136
Inconsistency 137
Incontinence, of faeces 21, 24, 135
Inhibition 24
Institutional care, statutory require-
     ments 164
Intellectual function 6
Intolerance 3
Invalid care allowance 172
Irresponsibility 136
Isolation 68

Joint planning 152
Joint training 158, 159

Kidman, Brenda 136, 137

Laundry service 87

Local authorities, responsibilities 163
Local Authority Social Services Act,
     1970 81
Local Government Act, 1929 80, 161
Local Government Act, 1972 82
Longitudinal studies 7
Lucidity, islands of 26, 110

Mania 33, 36, 41
Manic-depressive psychosis 33, 36
Marie Curie Nursing Foundation 88
Marital status 65
Meals services, 85, 199
Memory impairment 2, 3, 6
  in depression 32
Mental abnormality
  definition 6
  incidence 133
  pathology 8
  prevalence 7
  symptoms 133
Mental Health Act, 1959 36, 41, 126,
     165–7
  Section 25 127
  Section 26 130, 168
  Section 29 129
  Section 30 129
  Part VIII 169
Mental illness 6
Misplacement 154
Mobility allowance 173
Multi-disciplinary approach 159
Myocardial infarction 13

National Assistance Act, 1948 81, 82,
     94, 162, 165 ff.
  Section 47 122
National Assistance (Amendment) Act,
     1951 82
National Association for Mental Health
     152
National Council for the Single Woman
     and her Dependents 135
National Health Service Reorganisation
     Act, 1973 82
Neglect
  of cleanliness 2
  of feeding 2
  of mentally infirm old people 134
Neighbours, interviews with 117
Neurosis 30, 39
Newspaper test 27

Night duty service 92
Night relief 78
Night Watch Service 88
Noise, reduced tolerance of 33
Nursing homes 144

Occupational therapy 87
Operant conditioning 38
Overactivity 33
Over-protection 121

Paranoia 14, 39
Paraphrenia 37, 128
Perseveration 19, 25
Personality disorders 14, 43 ff.
  management of 47
Pet care 94
Physical illness 31
Placement 56
Pneumonia 13
Poor Law Amendment Act, 1834 80, 94
Population statistics 62 ff.
Power of Attorney 169
Pre-senile dementia 12
Prevention 50
Primary care 49
Probate 170
Psychiatric services 58
Psychiatric units 54, 55
Psychiatrists 115
  with special interest in the elderly
  157
Psychogeriatric units 56, 59, 154
Psychogeriatrics 58
Psychosis 30
Psychotherapy
  in neurosis 40
  in schizophrenia 38

Rate rebate 172
Reality Orientation Programmes 93
Red Cross 88
Referral procedure 83, 113
Register of old people 90
Registration and recall 22
Relatives
  conference 92
  help from 69, 70, 78
  interview with 117
Relief admission 59, 156
Religion, and suicide 35

Religious delusions, in schizophrenia
  38
Removal from home (*see also* Compulsory removal from home) 122
Rent Rebate 172
Research
  on brain failure 147
  on drugs 149
  on work of social workers 157
Residential accommodation 31, 94 ff.,
  119
  number of persons in 200
  statutory provisions 164
Residential care
  aims 97
  deprivation 151
Residential homes for the mentally
  disordered 95
Residential workers, training of 158
Resources 149
  allocation 155
  of Departments of Geriatric
    Medicine 52
Restlessness 33
Restriction of mobility 6
Retardation 32, 33
Retirement 31, 45
Risk 18, 125
Royal College of Psychiatrists 58
Royal National Institute for the Blind
  (RNIB) 88
'Running repairs help' 94

Safety 3
Schizophrenia 37
  prognosis 38
  treatment 38
  violence 41
Seebohm Report 81, 83
Senile dementia 135
Senile plaque disease 12
Senility 8
Sense of propriety 3
Sensory deprivation 6
*Services for Mental Illness Related to Old
  Age (HM (72) 71)* 55, 58
Set test 27
Sex distribution 64
Sexual aberration 24, 41
Sheltered Housing 96
Short-term care 156

Sleep
  disturbance 32
  loss of 135
Social services 80 ff.
Social Services Departments 83
  responsibilities 55
Speech disturbances
  in brain failure 13
  in depression 32
Strain on relatives 138, 141
Stripping 2, 24, 139
Stroke 10, 11
Stupor, depressive 33
Suicide 33, 34, 41
  attempted 41
  causes 35
  incidence 34, 35
Supplementary Benefits Commission 171
Supplementary pension 102, 171
Surveillance 50
Suspiciousness 39, 45, 116

Task Force 94
Telephones 108
Terminal care 93
Testamentary capacity 41, 170
Thyroid disease 13
Token economy 38
Trade Unions 158

Training
  of doctors 157
  of medical students 157
  of social workers 158
Tranquillizers 21
Transport concessions 172
Tumour of the brain 10
Turnover in Departments of Geriatric Medicine 57

Unconcern 2
'Universal Daughters' 91
Unworthiness, feelings of 33

Vigilance, diminution of 17
Violence 41, 135
Visiting services 86
Voluntary organizations 189
Voluntary workers 150, 158

Wandering 2, 21, 135
Wardens 96
Weight loss 32
Where's the Key? 136, 137
Widowhood 67, 93
Wills 170
Women's Royal Voluntary Service (WRVS) 85, 91
Words, misuse of 104 ff.